The Texaco Story

Faithfully Yours

1902   1952

for Fifty Years

The Texaco Story

The First Fifty Years

1902-1952

Written for The Texas Company

by MARQUIS JAMES

For narrative convenience in the text
of this book, distinction is not always
made between The Texas Company and
subsidiaries, and in some cases "The Texas
Company," "Texaco," or "the Company"
is used in a sense that either includes
subsidiaries or refers to subsidiaries.

1702।

CONTENTS

665.5

J23

Foreword

Since the years have a way of passing more quickly than we realize, it often takes a milestone to call our attention to the times, the places, and the people who have gone before.

On April 7, 1952, The Texas Company reached such a milestone. This was our Golden Anniversary.

Naturally, we are proud that during the past half century we have been a substantial contributor to improvements, new uses, and faster methods in producing, refining, transporting, and marketing petroleum. We are proud, as well, that we have played an important part in the industrial development of the nation.

Looking back, we are well aware that our history is brief against time, but the same 50 years in which we grew into one of the world's largest companies also produced profound political, social, economic, and technological changes that shaped the destiny of the world. Petroleum was a major factor among them. With each passing year, it has become increasingly vital to our economy and to the defense of the free world.

The tremendous strides of The Texas Company were due to the faith and energy of our past and present employes and stockholders. These men and women have come from all walks of life —they are scientists and laborers; they are housewives and financiers; they are next-door neighbors. On our Golden Anniversary, more than 40,000 employes and 115,000 stockholders stood behind The Texas Company.

This 50-year history is the story of, and a tribute to, teamwork. It is a story of progress, of five decades in which men and women of The Texas Company proved their industrial ingenuity and strength. It is also a story of risks and courage, physical and financial. Above all, it is the story of The Texas Company's participation in the miracle of oil.

We were fortunate in securing the services of Marquis James to write *The Texaco Story*, and we feel that the eminent Pulitzer Prize author and biographer has told our history vividly. With the aid of the Company's Public Relations staff, stories and legends of the early days were checked and evaluated, original documents were obtained, questions were asked and answered, facts sifted and compared. Mr. James has written the story of Texaco's first 50 years the way he sees it. He has selected from the vast compilation of research material that which he, as an outsider looking in on the Company, considers most pertinent and interesting. What emerges is a true story of an impressive era in our national history.

We wish to thank Louis Wiltz Kemp, former Texaco employe and a recognized authority on the history of the State of Texas, for the years of research that went into his factual, chronological history of The Texas Company. The data that he compiled now form part of the Company archives and were of valuable assistance to the author.

In presenting *The Texaco Story*, the Directors and Officers wish also to express their gratitude to employes, shareholders, customers, and the many other individuals and firms who have contributed to the success of The Texas Company, and to stress their belief that the next 50 years will produce even greater miracles of oil.

THE TEXAS COMPANY

I.

1902-1913

The Frontier
Years

Joseph S. Cullinan

Director, April 7, 1902—November 25, 1913
President, May 20, 1902—November 25, 1913

Joseph Stephen Cullinan was born in Sharon, Pennsylvania, December 31, 1860. In 1882, he went to work for Standard Oil in Oil Creek, Pennsylvania, and in 1895 organized the Petroleum Iron Works in the same state. His interest in oil led him to Corsicana, Texas, in 1897, where he established an oil refinery and later organized the Texas Fuel Company, predecessor of The Texas Company. He also was instrumental in organizing Producers Oil Company, which The Texas Company absorbed. He was an officer and a director of Producers, as well as president and a director of the Texas Fuel Company and of a number of The Texas Company's early subsidiaries. After he left The Texas Company, he organized the first unit of what became the American Republics Corporation. He died in Palo Alto, California, March 11, 1937, while on a visit to the West Coast.

1. Two Men Create a Company

"Buckskin Joe" and the New York financier
see farther and truer than most,
and they have the talent for the job

The Texas Company is the only oil company that sells its products directly in all the 48 states. Moreover, the Company and its associated companies sell products throughout most of the world, excluding Soviet Russia and Communist-dominated areas. The Texas Company is also remarkable in other ways. With assets of $1,549,000,000 at the beginning of 1952, it ranks fourth among the oil companies of the United States. Only three companies—Standard Oil Company (New Jersey), Standard Oil Company (Indiana), and Socony-Vacuum Oil Company, Incorporated—are larger. These companies and other so-called "Standard" companies compete with one another. Therefore, to lump them together as the "Standard group," and to lump together other companies as the "independent group," is to convey an impression that is no longer true. The oil business is a competitive business all around. So-called independents compete among themselves, they compete with Standard companies, and Standard companies compete just as vigorously among themselves.

That was far from the case, however, in 1902, when The Texas Company got its start. Standard did 80 per cent of the nation's oil business and a greater percentage abroad. The independents, scrambling for what was left, found the going tough and risky. Few of them lasted very long or went very far. In this dog-eat-dog environment The Texas Company not only survived, it throve—almost from the word go.

While independent contemporaries perished on every hand, The Texas Company throve because of the force, the sagacity, and the unremitting energy of two men, Joseph Stephen Cullinan and Arnold Schlaet.

Cullinan and Schlaet were dissimilar men by origin, temperament, and training. The wonder is that they worked together as long and as well as they did. Cullinan came up from the bottom in the Pennsylvania oil fields, on the edge of which he was born. In his young days they called him "Buckskin Joe," and he could get more work out of a gang of men than almost anyone. Men liked him because he was a leader and not a driver. His name has survived as one of the giants among the pioneers of the petroleum industry in the Southwest.

Schlaet's has not. Only a careful combing of old records and correspondence that have been gathering dust for nearly 50 years establishes his great importance to The Texas Company. Arnold Schlaet was born in Germany. His English was good, almost too good. He had no nickname. He was no mixer. There was always a bit of Continental remoteness in his manner. Though he became a thorough-going oil man, he did not begin at the bottom, like Cullinan. He never bossed a gang of men in the field. He came into the business as an investor, and his indispensable service to The Texas Company was in the realm of sales and finance. Schlaet had some good ideas about field operations, too, and he passed them on to Cullinan to carry out. He found much of the money Cullinan needed for his work. These two men supplemented each other and helped the young Company get along.

So, taken together, Cullinan and Schlaet made a great pair. At a critical juncture, and amid a world of distractions, they saw farther and saw truer into the cloudy future of the business than most other men among the independents.

Cullinan and Schlaet were undoubtedly among the first to see the possibilities of the ownership of crude oil reserves in the prolific fields being discovered in Texas and Louisiana as a basis on which to build and compete successfully with the Standard Oil

Arnold Schlaet

Director, April 7, 1902—January 1, 1920
First Vice President, May 20, 1902—November 17, 1914

Arnold Schlaet was born in Germany in 1859 and came to the United States in 1875. As an employe of H. G. Lapham and Co., he managed that investment firm's interests in oil and carbon black. This led to a meeting with J. S. Cullinan when the oil boom struck Beaumont, Texas, in 1901. The two men were the prime movers in creating The Texas Company. Mr. Schlaet's chief contributions were in finance and sales in the eastern United States and in Europe. For 18 years he took an active part in the affairs of The Texas Company, and for many more years he exercised considerable influence. Mr. Schlaet died at his Winter home in St. Petersburg, Florida, November 14, 1946.

Company. Up to about that time, Standard had been content to be primarily a buyer of crude oil and to be a refining, transporting, and marketing company. Standard was satisfied to leave crude oil production to independent producers. Standard's buying policy on crude oil was based on the law of supply and demand.

Cullinan and Schlaet saw that the opening of the Texas and other southwestern oil fields would alter the geographical pattern of the industry. They saw new uses for oil. Until 1900, the principal use was for lighting—kerosine for lamps. After 1900, oil as a source of power came into its own, first as a replacement of coal as fuel for industrial plants and steam locomotives. J. S. Cullinan was the first man in Texas to fuel a locomotive with oil. By 1910, the rise of the automobile was stimulating the market for gasoline, for which there had been virtually no sale 10 years before. Presently it was outselling all other petroleum products.

Sound ideas as to the changing nature of the oil business, reasonably adequate finances with which to launch a new enterprise calculated to take advantage of those ideas: these are important ingredients for success. They cannot, however, insure success. An instrument, a *company*, must be created, and it must be managed. That takes a special talent. Cullinan and Schlaet had it. They created The Texas Company and they outlined and directed its operations under trying conditions. The Texas oil booms, touched off by the Lucas gusher on Spindletop in 1901, started a chain of events which brought the small predecessor of The Texas Company (and some 200 rivals) into being, and precipitated scenes that have been compared with those of the California gold rush and the Klondike. Men played things on the short run. Fortunes were made and lost in a day. Amid this rough-and-tumble, level heads were required to hold to the long view, and to hold together a working force, a *company*, in the face of temptations to try for quicker rewards. Cullinan did it. A surprising number of the pioneering employes, who slept in their clothes and worked around the clock in the days when drinking water in the Spindletop field sold for 10 cents a cup and oil for three cents a barrel, stuck with The Texas Company until it emerged as a factor in the nation's petroleum industry.

But we are ahead of our story.

Among the Original Directors of The Texas Company

R. E. Brooks
Lawyer
Beaumont, Texas

William T. Campbell
Banker and Publisher
Beaumont, Texas

John W. Gates
Financier
Chicago, Illinois

J. C. Hutchins
Lawyer
Chicago, Illinois

Lewis H. Lapham
Industrialist
New York City

E. J. Marshall
Banker
Beaumont, Texas

Roderick Oliver
Banker
Beaumont, Texas

IN 1902, WHEN FIRE THREATENED SPINDLETOP FIELD, JOSEPH S. CULLINAN SAVED THE DAY

BEFORE THE OIL BOOM IN 1903, SOUR LAKE WAS WELL KNOWN FOR ITS CURATIVE WATERS

2. "Buy It in Texas, Sell It Up North"

The boom at Spindletop gives Mr. Cullinan an idea;
Mr. Schlaet helps find the capital,
and The Texas Company is in business

Joseph S. Cullinan had learned the oil business in the best school in the world at the time—the Rockefeller, or Standard, school in northwestern Pennsylvania. There the industry had been born, in 1859, when a well drilled by a former railroad conductor named Drake came in at 69 and one-half feet. The initial production was 25 barrels a day. John D. Rockefeller achieved a semblance of order in the industry long before the end of the Nineteenth Century. He changed the processing and marketing of petroleum from a gamble to a business.

Cullinan went to work for the Standard Oil Company in Pennsylvania in 1882, the year he was old enough to vote. By that time, the oil industry was the fastest growing industry in the United States, and already was dominated by Rockefeller as no other great American industry has ever been dominated by one man. Still, Standard was young and small enough for a subordinate to get an all-around education. Cullinan remained with Standard for 13 years. At the end of this time, he could drill a well, put up a tank farm, lay a pipe line, or run a refinery.

In 1895, he left Standard and two years later established himself at Corsicana, in eastern Texas, where a small field had been discovered. The young enterpriser formed a partnership called J. S. Cullinan & Company, which was not quite independent of Standard. Silent partners and providers of much of the capital were two Standard officials, Henry C. Folger

and Calvin N. Payne. Quickly, J. S. Cullinan & Company became the largest and most prosperous operator in the Corsicana
field. A tank farm was erected, and oil bought from well owners.
It was sold to refiners and marketers, principally Standard, and
carried away in railroad tank cars. At a cost of $150,000, Cul-
linan built a refinery, the first worthy of the name west of the
Mississippi. The refinery produced kerosine for lamps, the use
for petroleum that exceeded all other uses combined. There was
so little use for gasoline, an unavoidable by-product of the manufacture of kerosine and lubricating oils, that most of it was
thrown away. Yet, Cullinan's mind was busy with the prospect
of new uses for oil products. He himself tested crude oil for fuel
on a specially fitted locomotive of the St. Louis & Southwestern
Railroad. The test was successful. He laid the dust of Corsicana's
unpaved streets by sprinkling oil on them, another innovation.

Still, Cullinan was not satisfied. Prospects around Corsicana
were limited by the output of the local field, which remained
small. Wells were being drilled, however, at other places in
Texas. Cullinan kept an eye on them. He intended to move in
wherever sufficient oil should be found to make it worth while.

A mining engineer named Anthony F. Lucas was "boring"
(as the word was in those days) a well on Spindletop Hill, a few
miles south of Beaumont and a few miles north of the newly
created town of Port Arthur, southern terminus of the Kansas
City Southern Railroad, which had recently pushed its line to
the Gulf.

Spindletop can be called a hill only by comparison with
the flatness of the surrounding coastal plain. It is a gentle rise
that may be as much as 10 feet high.

Without oil, that part of Texas was prospering—on lumber, rice, and cattle. John W. Gates of Chicago, who held a stock
interest in the Kansas City Southern Railroad, had commercial
interests in Port Arthur and visited there frequently. A combination of gambler and constructive industrialist, "Bet-a-Mil-
lion" Gates was one of the remarkable figures of his era. His
American Steel & Wire Company had gone into the gigantic

combine that was to become the world's first billion-dollar corporation, United States Steel. Later, in a tussle with J. P. Morgan, Gates' wings and assets were trimmed considerably. The story was that Morgan exiled the Chicagoan from Wall Street. However that may have been, in 1900 Gates still had a few millions to invest.

On January 10, 1901, an underground explosion that was heard for miles stopped the "boring" at the Lucas well. Mud shot into the air. Then came a geyser of oil, spouting twice the height of the derrick. There had been gushers in oil fields before, but never a gusher like this.

Joseph S. Cullinan arrived on the scene a few days later. He did not arrive alone. Already the countryside was thronged with sightseers and speculators. The geyser still spouted. From 70,000 to 100,000 barrels of oil a day were running down the gentle slopes of Spindletop. At 80 or 90 cents a barrel, which oil brought north of the Ohio River, this represented a large waste of money. The first problem was to cap the well. It took 10 days to do the job.

By that time, the boom was on. Beaumont's former population of 8,000 had nearly doubled. On the day the well was capped, one special train brought 2,500 persons from Houston alone. Invaders slept in chairs and on floors. The town's drinking water nearly gave out. Some say it was as cheap to drink whisky and probably more healthful. Saloons, honky-tonks, and gambling houses materialized overnight. As matters turned out, faro banks provided one of the more conservative forms of investment in Beaumont in 1901 and 1902.

One's chance of winning at faro was as good as in all but a half-dozen of the 200 oil companies that bloomed to exploit the Spindletop field. Few of the promoters, and almost none of the suckers, had ever seen an oil well before. Leases around Spindletop went for incredible prices. Drilling equipment weighing tons was shipped *by express* from places as distant as Pittsburgh, this despite the fact that more production was the last thing needed at Spindletop—for the time being, that is. The first thing was

FROM THE FIRST BEAUMONT OFFICES . . .

. . . A MOVE WAS MADE TO THIS BUILDING

TEXACO'S OFFICE BUILDING IN HOUSTON

TEXACO HEADQUARTERS IN NEW YORK CITY

WESTERN HEADQUARTERS, LOS ANGELES

to find ways of getting the oil to the refineries. Already this obstacle had driven the price of oil down to as low as three cents a barrel at the well.

The J. M. Guffey Petroleum Company, the corporate name under which Lucas and his partners operated, with the backing of the Mellon interests of Pittsburgh, was taking energetic steps to build a man-sized oil company on the strength of the Spindletop strike. The Mellons and some of their friends put in more money. The Guffey company began to lay a pipe line to Port Arthur and to build docks and a refinery there. They bought additional oil leases, amounting to a million acres, in Texas and Louisiana. Clearly, the Guffey people were out to challenge Rockefeller's Standard.

J. S. Cullinan seems to have had the same idea, but he could not go about its realization in the big way that Guffey was doing. He decided to begin by buying oil cheaply in Texas and selling it at a profit to Standard and other northern refiners. For that purpose, he formed, on paper, a few weeks after the Lucas strike, a concern called the Texas Fuel Company. The capitalization was only $50,000. Cullinan's Standard Oil partners in the Corsicana enterprise did not come in.

The first noteworthy support for the Texas Fuel Company came from a group of Texans operating under the name of the Hogg-Swayne Syndicate. This backing, in the form of properties valued at $25,000, was just half of what Cullinan needed to make his Texas Fuel Company a going concern. The Hogg-Swayne crowd needed Cullinan, the practical oil man, as badly as Cullinan needed capital.

The head of the syndicate was James Stephen Hogg, a former Governor of Texas, and one of the state's influential and picturesque figures. Hogg's associates were mostly lawyers. Like certain other novices, most of whom were to lose their investments, the Hogg people had gone in deep. For $105,000 they had bought land on Spindletop from a man who had paid $450 for the property a year before. Half of the tract was split into minute segments, some of them barely large enough to hold a derrick and drilling equipment. These "doormats" were sold for fancy prices, but usually not for cash. Purchasers were expected to pay from the profits of their oil wells. The collapse of the price of Texas crude made this difficult. Hogg-Swayne also had bought land for a pump station at Spindletop and for a refinery at Port Arthur. They had bought storage tanks and started to lay a pipe line from Spindletop to Port Arthur. Thus, heavily involved in undertakings they knew too little about, Hogg and his associates turned to the experienced Cullinan. A swap was made. Hogg-Swayne transferred a part of their holdings to the Texas Fuel Company for $25,000 worth of stock in it.

Cullinan got his remaining $25,000 from an unexpected source, and in the bargain he got Arnold Schlaet.

Schlaet was a trusted employe of John J. and Lewis H. Lapham, leather merchants of New York with several outside interests, including oil wells in Kansas and Pennsylvania. Schlaet concerned himself with the outside interests, and he virtually managed the Lapham brothers' oil business. Like every other oil-man in 1901, Schlaet wondered if he could make some money in Beaumont. He sent his field superintendent, Charles S. Miller, down to have a look. Miller had known Cullinan in the Pennsylvania fields. He liked Cullinan's Texas plans, and wired Schlaet himself to come down from New York.

Schlaet, too, gained a respect for Cullinan as a practical oil-man, and he liked his plan to buy oil cheap in Texas and sell it in the North at a profit; and then, gradually, to develop an all-around oil company as Guffey was doing. There was one detail of Cullinan's scheme that Schlaet didn't go along with; at any rate, he considered it premature. As the Texas Fuel Company was not chartered to produce oil—that is, drill wells—Cullinan wanted to organize an affiliated producing company. Schlaet contended that there was too much production already. The Fuel Company would have its hands full marketing the oil that others were bringing out of the ground.

So it was that on January 2, 1902, the Texas Fuel Company, with little cash at its disposal, went into business. Cullinan and Schlaet moved fast. For $39,695, they bought from the Hogg-Swayne Syndicate land for a refinery site at Port Arthur, two tanks, and a quantity of pipe for a line from the field to Port Arthur. That did not leave much cash. They went right on, however, to construct the pipe line, buy more land, and more tanks—in all making appropriations for expenditures aggregating more than $600,000.

Schlaet returned East, and in Texas the farsighted Cullinan had his way about a producing company. Without Schlaet's help or blessing, he organized the Producers Oil Company as an affiliate of the Texas Fuel Company. Gates and other prominent men came into Producers. That these men chose to join Cullinan speaks well for Cullinan. Among a host of new companies that had sprung into being with the widely advertised purpose of making millions out of Spindletop oil, they had had many opportunities for investment. Gates and his associates bore names that were an asset to any new company, and Gates was one of the bold and imaginative promoters of his day. What these men did not know was the oil business. They relied on Cullinan for that.

Gates was not a man to be content with an investment in a mere affiliate. Consequently, he and his friends and his son, Charles, accepted "certificates of interest" in the Texas Fuel Company. These certificates were a device by which Schlaet and Cullinan got promises of financial support for the Fuel Company without committing the promisers to much. Schlaet saw to it that the investments of the Gates group would not be enough to carry control. Gates and associates came in for about $90,000. The "certificates of interest" totaled around $450,000.

The Texas Fuel Company, capitalized at $50,000, was far too small an organization to carry out the grand plans of Cullinan and Schlaet. Accordingly, in March, 1902, it was arranged that a new corporation, called The Texas Company, should take over the assets of the Fuel Company. These assets were reckoned at $1,250,000, although they had not cost nearly that much. This proved to be a very conservative valuation for what Cullinan had picked up, largely on credit. The capital of The Texas Company was to be $3,000,000, of which $1,650,000 would be paid in. On April 7, 1902, the charter of The Texas Company was filed with the Secretary of State of Texas, and the future billion-and-a-half-dollar corporation was in business.

Cullinan was President. Arnold Schlaet was elected First Vice President. Gates became a Director. Actually, for the time being, everything revolved about Cullinan. What investors were buying was his leadership. It was needed, for the Beaumont boom had reached fantastic proportions. Wells were going down all over, nearly all of them producers. In 1902, 18,515,000 barrels of oil were produced in the State of Texas, giving it second place, next to Ohio, among the oil producing states. All but a million barrels of this Texas oil came from Spindletop.

A dramatic incident underlined the respect that competitors, as well as Texas Company shareholders, had for the leadership of J. S. Cullinan. On a Sunday in September, 1902, one of the Spindletop wells caught fire. The flames spread to other wells, jammed against one another as the rigs were. The entire field, the richest producing oil field in the world, was threatened. Anxious city officials of Beaumont, influential citizens, and oil operators met to deal with the crisis. Cullinan was present. He always tried to spend Sundays with his family in Corsicana, but this Sunday he had been unable to get away. The meeting appealed to the President of The Texas Company to take charge of the fire fighting. Cullinan accepted, with the understanding that he should have complete authority over men and property in the field, authority that he could enforce with a pistol if necessary.

The leader took the same risks as the men he commanded. When the fire had been put out, he staggered back to his buggy almost blind from gas fumes.

Schlaet, in New York, busy selling stock to raise funds for Cullinan's operations, was disturbed by his partner's indifference to danger. After a second fire, Schlaet wrote anxiously that he hoped Cullinan had taken no undue risks:

"The investment down there will . . . lose every attraction for us should you be disabled."

3. The First Year
Is a Big Year

*The new Company contracts for a million barrels of oil
and buys the equipment to handle it,
finds markets, takes a profitable gamble at Sour Lake,
and declares its first dividend*

In the same forthright way that he dealt with oil fires, J. S. Cullinan administered the expanding affairs of The Texas Company. There was activity on every hand. Already, many of the oil ventures that Spindletop brought into being had collapsed. Many more were to do so. Today, only one large company besides Texaco traces its beginnings directly to Spindletop. This is Gulf (the name taken by Guffey late in 1901). In 1902, Gulf was doing more and spending more than Texaco.

Nevertheless, The Texas Company finished the pipe line started by the Hogg-Swayne people. It ran from Spindletop to the nearby railway loading stations of Garrison and Nederland, and on to the Company's refinery site and dock at Port Arthur. The line was laid by Jack Ennis, who had spent a lifetime in oil fields. Although he could not sign his name, Jack Ennis had no superior as the boss of a pipe line crew. The Texas Company built 15 steel tanks at Garrison, 12 at Nederland, seven at Port Arthur, and two at Amesville, Louisiana, across the river from New Orleans. It built an earthen tank with a capacity of 103,000 barrels. These tanks were filled with oil, some of which was bought for as little as three and five cents per barrel, the lowest prices, before or since, in the industry's history. The Company bought 10 tank cars and a 400-foot wooden vessel, *Texas Barge No. 1*, to move oil from Port Arthur to the Amesville terminal. It began the construction of a $150,000 refinery and a $20,000 asphalt plant at Port Arthur. In all, by the end of 1902, when The Texas Company was eight months old, it had invested $652,040.70, and was committed to additional heavy outlays.

This activity went on amid pioneering conditions that are picturesque to look back upon, but were rather trying to live through. Beaumont was still a camp, swarming, as one old-timer with The Texas Company recalls, with "sightseers, speculators, honky-tonk hostesses, salesmen, peddlers, lawyers, bartenders, doctors, farmers, gamblers, miners, bankers, newspapermen, oilmen from the East, promoters, tramps, people honestly seeking employment, and people of many other sorts." Many substantial citizens sent their families elsewhere, kept one room to sleep in, and rented out the others at fancy prices. Shacks and tents were everywhere. Saloons and gambling houses never closed. In dry weather, dust from the unpaved streets filled the air and settled over everything. In wet weather, the streets were rivers of mud.

The first offices of The Texas Company were in Beaumont, Texas, and consisted of three rooms in a corrugated iron structure close to the Southern Pacific depot, directly across the street from the Southern Pacific tracks. In the Fall of 1902, the Company was lucky enough to get quarters in the town's most imposing edifice, the three-story brick Temperance Hall Building. The eastern office consisted of one room in the Maritime Building, at 8 Bridge Street, New York, rented for $35 a month and equipped with furniture costing $161.28. This was the headquarters of First Vice President Arnold Schlaet.

The Beaumont office force and The Texas Company workers from the field who had business in Beaumont seem to have fared better in their domestic living arrangements than most oil company personnel in those early days. They slept and ate at a large residence which the Company had leased and called the Texas Club. Some of the men's wives came down to relieve the bachelor nature of the atmosphere. When in Beaumont, Cullinan stayed at the Texas Club, and brought his business guests there. For $1,050, the Company bought a launch, which was rechristened the *Texas Girl*, and used mainly for pleasure by the employes. Forty years later, Company pioneers who had attained prominence in the industry were to recall with a reminiscent glow the delights of Sunday picnics aboard the *Texas Girl*.

By the end of 1902, the Company's sales program was taking shape. It sold oil to northern refiners and to sugar plantations in Louisiana for use as fuel in grinding operations. A few sales to plantations, and the hope of increasing that business, were responsible for the establishment of the Amesville terminal. Cullinan learned that Louisiana sugar planters consumed 450,000 tons of coal a year. This was about equivalent to 1,350,000 barrels of oil. Oil at a dollar a barrel would represent a saving in fuel costs to the planter, and a fine profit to the oil dealer. With the opening of transportation facilities, the price of oil at the well in Spindletop had recovered somewhat, but the average for the year 1902 was still 21 cents a barrel.

All the ambitious plans of The Texas Company depended on a plentiful supply of oil from the Southeast Texas wells, which, in 1902, meant Spindletop. The Texas Company had contracted with its affiliate, Producers, to supply a million barrels at 25 cents per barrel. Producers set forth in a large way to fulfill this contract. Fifteen acres, on which there were big producing wells, were bought for $120,000. Then, in the Fall of the year, the wells ceased to flow. Pumping, an expensive operation, was resorted to. Oil men believed the wells could be restored by "blowing" with compressed air. Producers ordered blowing equipment, and, still optimistic, contracted for six brand new wells at $6,000 apiece.

The hopes based on these moves collapsed like a punctured balloon. Before the costly air plant could be assembled, salt water invaded the Spindletop wells. The miracle field's production dropped from 62,000 barrels a day to 20,000, and within another year it was down to 5,000. Spindletop was done for until, 20-odd years later, oilmen would discover a deeper formation. Without fresh sources of oil, The Texas Company also would be done for.

The oil was found, and dramatically enough on property

PUMPING STATION AT SOUR LAKE, 1904

OILMEN LIVED AT THE SOUR LAKE HOTEL

A SECOND-HAND LAUNCH, RECHRISTENED *TEXAS GIRL*, WAS MUCH IN DEMAND FOR OUTINGS

which The Texas Company had an option to buy—at Sour Lake, about 20 miles northwest of doomed Spindletop. Even before the Spindletop strike, Cullinan had been watching Sour Lake, where prospectors had found oil in small quantities. As the Spindletop boom progressed, Cullinan thought enough of Sour Lake to take, in the name of The Texas Company, an option on an 865-acre tract priced at $1,000,000. For the option, The Texas Company paid $20,000 cash. A part of the arrangement was that three test wells be drilled. The first two found some oil. The third blew in as a gusher on January 8, 1903, two years almost to the day after the Lucas strike at Spindletop, and a few months after the appearance of the salt water that was to ruin that field and menace the prospects of The Texas Company.

Sour Lake restored the Company's fortunes, but this required bold and decisive action. The option was about to expire, and a million dollars had to be laid on the line. The Company sought to raise it by disposing of additional Texas Company stock. John W. Gates said that he and some friends would take $590,-000 of the new stock. He offered to put up the whole million, if need be, to be repaid when other subscribers were found. There was no need to take advantage of Mr. Gates' generosity. The Lapham group came in for $350,000. Others came in until the fund was oversubscribed—especially since the Company was able to close for $900,000, because of a possible flaw in the title.

The Texas Company's Sour Lake gusher helped touch off a boom that was a repetition of Spindletop, on a smaller scale. Nor was that all. In the year 1903, oil was found in nearby Saratoga and Batson, Texas, and in Jennings, Louisiana. The Batson and Saratoga strikes were small, but Jennings was another bonanza, its production in 1904 almost equaling that of Spindletop in its best year, 1902. At all these new fields, The Texas Company was in on the ground floor through the Producers Oil Company and other affiliates. Producers bounced back from its Spindletop fiasco, and, with other affiliates, made welcome profits for the parent company.

With next to no oil coming in during the last weeks of 1902, by the middle of 1903 The Texas Company was swimming in oil, thanks to the Sour Lake gamble. That year, The Texas Company brought 3,813,000 barrels of petroleum from the ground, or about four per cent of the total production of the United States. In 1904, The Texas Company's production was 5,501,000 barrels, or 4.7 per cent of the national yield. From almost nothing, it had come abreast of the country's leaders in production.

Three months after the Sour Lake strike, The Texas Company was on firm enough ground to declare its first dividend—$165,000. Net profits for the 12 months ending April 30, 1903, were $303,036, leaving, after dividends, a tidy sum for the development of the business. On April 30, 1904, the close of the Company's second year, profits were $794,250, and dividends, $180,000. Every year thereafter, to the present time, The Texas Company has paid its shareholders a dividend.

Desirable as dividends are in the eyes of stockholders, a good deal more important to the welfare of the young company in 1903 and 1904 was the general development of the business. The Texas Company had the oil. The thing to do was to market it. That was the big undertaking, and the one to which Arnold Schlaet gave a large part of his attention. The impetus toward sales, which was to play an important rôle in the early climb of The Texas Company, came in the main from the little office in Bridge Street, New York, and Schlaet was responsible for it.

The first sales of the Company were of crude oil and asphalt. A few orders for asphalt were received before The Texas Company's asphalt plant was in operation. They were filled by buying the product from the Gulf refinery, the first refinery to get going in Port Arthur. An asphalt salesman in St. Louis, named George M. Brown, in 1902, first used the word "Texaco" as a product name. It had originated in Schlaet's New York office as a cable address. In 1906, the Company registered the name as a trade mark. In 1909, the Texaco red star with the green "T" appeared.

During the Company's first two years, the only profits worth mentioning came from the sale of crude oil for fuel to the

Mississippi River sugar planters, and to other oil companies with northern refineries, and to railroads. Such sales kept The Texas Company afloat, and provided money for expansion and for dividends. The Company was able to do this because it got the jump on most other outfits in providing storage and transportation facilities. By 1905, Texaco had four tankers, and it had made arrangements with barge lines to carry crude from the Company's dock at Port Arthur to New Orleans. Thus, with transportation facilities available, the Company was able to buy surplus oil in eastern Texas and move it to market.

Late in 1903, the Company's refinery at Port Arthur began operations. The practice of the day was that a refinery must make what the salesmen could sell. This is what other oil companies were doing—manufacturing products easy to make and easy to sell, and discarding unwanted by-products, such as gasoline and asphalt.

Texaco's analytical management eventually saw a way to improve on this principle. It determined to make *all* of every barrel of crude into products that would bring the greatest profit. This was a sound policy. It helped make Texaco a leader instead of a company that followed what the rest of the industry was doing. It stimulated the selling forces to find new markets, kept sales and refining people coöperating and watching costs, and helped pay Texaco's dividends down through the years.

In 1903, the largest selling retail petroleum product was kerosine, used principally in lamps and cooking stoves. Sour Lake and Louisiana crude did not produce the best grade of kerosine. It was not very good for lamps. Consequently, Texaco did not go in heavily for kerosine. During the early years, the principal product of its first refinery was what the trade called "gas oil." It was used to enrich artificial gas used for lighting and cooking in cities all over the United States and in Europe. With this product was begun The Texas Company's export trade.

The Port Arthur refinery also turned out a fair quantity of gasoline, most of it a low-grade product by present standards, called naphtha. Naphtha was used for cooking stoves, illuminat-

PORT ARTHUR TERMINAL WAS BUILT CLOSE BY PORT ARTHUR WORKS...

...AND HAS GROWN TO BE THE COMPANY'S LARGEST SHIPPING POINT

ing torches, industrial engines, and as a solvent for paints. For the better grades of gasoline there was not much of a market. One use for this gasoline was to run the noisy, smelly, and temperamental little engines used to propel automobiles. Neither The Texas Company nor any other oil company was yet paying too much attention to this. Few dreamed that the horseless carriage someday would actually supplant the horse.

In 1907, as we shall see in more detail presently, Texaco began to bring Oklahoma crude by pipe line to Texas. This was marvelous oil. It made twice as much kerosine as Texas oil and five times as much gasoline. Moreover, it made better lamp oil than Texas crude. By that time, Texaco had a refinery in operation at West Dallas, more convenient than Port Arthur to the supply of Oklahoma oil. The Company introduced its Familylite, a superior grade of illuminating oil. Selling it was another thing. The *sub rosa* Standard Oil subsidiary, Waters-Pierce, controlled the kerosine market in the Southwest.

So it was that the Texaco tank wagons found hard going at first with their Familylite. With kerosine of the stove grade they did better. Within a few years, however, The Texas Company was able to establish its Familylite and, later, Crystalite, as successful competitors of the Standard products. This was accomplished by alert salesmanship and by rendering better service to the retailer. Standard had had its own way so long that it had grown careless in these particulars. Moreover, the monopolistic nature of the great company itself had tended to make it unpopular.

The entry of The Texas Company into Philadelphia furnishes an example of how it profited by Standard's oversights. Once a week only did the Standard tank wagons make deliveries of kerosine to hardware and grocery stores, which were the principal retailers. This was inconvenient for the retailers, who were nearly all small concerns with limited facilities for storing oil. The result was that many emptied their tanks within a few days, and had no kerosine for their customers until the Standard wagon appeared again, after an absence of a week. Consequently, The

Texas Company inaugurated twice-a-week deliveries. Finding dealers with empty tanks, they got a good many orders that would not have been theirs otherwise. When Standard began making two deliveries a week, Texaco made them every other day. Presently, daily deliveries were the rule with both companies, but by that time, The Texas Company was well established in Philadelphia.

The Texas Company showed similar alertness in the gasoline field. It sold its gasoline in an ever-expanding market which had begun to respond to the fact that the horseless carriage was here to stay. The number of passenger cars on the roads increased from 23,000 in 1902, the year Texaco was born, to 902,000 in 1912, and the number of trucks from none to 41,000. Gasoline sales in the United States mounted from 5,787,000 barrels to 20,300,000 in the same period. The automobile was the largest single factor in this increase. In 1909, with superior Oklahoma crude at its disposal, The Texas Company recognized this new and growing market by turning out at its West Dallas refinery what it called No. 4 Motor Gasoline. Aware that here was a chance to ride the crest of a mounting wave, Texaco stepped up its gasoline production. It sold every gallon it refined. The conquest of the difficult kerosine market became less important. By 1914, and maybe earlier, The Texas Company was making and selling more motor fuel than kerosine, being probably the first company thus to demonstrate the shape of things to come, and come soon, in the oil industry.

The filling station and the filling-station pump, the badges of an oil company destined to become most familiar to the average American, came into being by a process of fairly swift evolution. At first, the motorist filled the tank of his machine by means of a can and a funnel. Most of the gasoline was so likely to be contaminated with dirt that it worked best if strained through a piece of chamois. The quality of gasoline was improved, and also the method of getting it into an automobile. Soon, a motorist could drive into a garage, where an attendant filled his tank from a barrel with a hand pump and hose. Then came the underground storage tank, and, about 1910, the pump at the curbstone. These curbstone pumps are recognizable as the forerunners of the service station pump of today.

A selling organization, handling the various products of the Company's refineries, developed something like Topsy; it "just growed." At first, Cullinan, with everything else he had to do, took care of sales in the South and West, and Schlaet handled them in the East. Then the busy Cullinan entrusted all but the railroad accounts to others. By then, fuel oil was a product of the refineries, and much better in performance than the raw crude. The Navy began to use it, in 1912 buying 15,000,000 gallons from The Texas Company and, in 1913, 25,000,000 gallons.

Sales activities had been carried on in the early years, as we have seen, both from the Company's headquarters in Texas and from New York. In 1907, Texaco organized a central sales division. By 1908, all the nation except five western states was covered by a sales organization with seven divisions. In 1910, Texaco maintained 229 distributing stations and agencies, all bearing the newly designed Texaco red star with the green "T." No other independent company operated over so large an area. In this way, The Texas Company rendered itself less vulnerable to Standard competition. When an independent was crowded into one territory, as most of them were, Standard could make things hot for it by cutting prices in that territory. A widely distributed company, like Texaco, could not be injured much by this practice. But competition there was, in spite of occasional loose statements that Texaco was a branch of Standard Oil. In 1907, a Texaco attorney named Amos L. Beaty answered one charge thus:

"The Texas Company was organized under the general laws of Texas in 1902 by those who are in the main its present stockholders. From that time to this day there has never been a moment of time when the Standard Oil Company directly or indirectly owned or controlled or had any interest in the stock or any part thereof or in its business otherwise."

1913—SOUTH AFRICA WAS AN OVERSEAS MARKET WHERE TEXACO PRODUCTS WERE SOLD

THE RED STAR WITH THE GREEN "T" EARLY BECAME WELL KNOWN IN FAR-OFF TASMANIA

In the last six months of 1910, the Company spent $16,222 on advertising—an amount which would not buy one page in *Life* magazine today. The products featured were Familylite kerosine for lamps, automobile gasoline, and Texaco roofing. Roofing was a product of the Company's asphalt works.

The Company began to develop the foreign retail market in 1905. Arnold Schlaet went to Europe and established the first sales agencies. Under his knowing guidance they flourished. In 1908, the new tanker *Texas*, one of the largest built at that time, went into regular service between Port Arthur and Continental ports. By 1913, the Texaco star was visible at agencies in Europe, Latin America, Australia, Africa, and several countries in Asia, including China. The principal products sold were kerosine, gas oil, lubricating oil, and fuel oil.

So much, in a very general way, for sales in the pioneering days of Texaco. To place the finished products in the salesmen's hands was not a simple undertaking to be gone about hit or miss. The work that lay behind sales had to be organized to a high degree, and rather delicately balanced. This required money in large amounts, and, just as important as money, it required men, men with know-how and driving energy exerted in the right directions at the right times. Roughly summarized, this effort embraced the production of crude petroleum, the transportation and refining of it, and the distribution of the refined products. Activity toward these ends expanded in widening circles. A dozen things in a dozen departments were going on every minute, and everything had to fit together.

As for production, Cullinan looked not to current requirements alone; he also anticipated future needs on what some thought to be an overly optimistic scale. Texaco got in on all the great new southwestern strikes—the Humble field, near Houston, early in 1905; Glenn Pool, near the village of Tulsa, in the Creek Nation of the Indian Territory, in December of that year; the Goose Creek and Markham fields, near Houston, in 1908. Between 1903 and 1912, The Texas Company's gross production ran from 3,800,000 to 8,000,000 barrels annually.

In 1913, it jumped to 10,420,000, which was more than four per cent of the country's production.

Nearly all the drilling operations of The Texas Company were conducted by its affiliate, the Producers Oil Company, of which Walter Bedford Sharp was president and guiding genius. It was the ability of Sharp that placed Texaco in the front rank of oil producers.

In 1912, Sharp died, at the age of 42. So passed a great oilman whose work has left its impress not on The Texas Company alone, but on the entire industry. Old-timers in the industry have related that Walter Sharp was drilling water wells near Dallas in the middle '90's, using mud to keep the holes from caving— a technique that has become standard practice in drilling oil wells to prevent cave-ins and to help control gas pressure. Sharp also helped develop a bit for cutting hard rock, and, with Howard Hughes of Texas, established the Sharp-Hughes Company for its manufacture. After the death of Walter Sharp, the Producers company was carried on successfully by others.

The important oil strike of the period was at Glenn Pool, destined to transform Tulsa into one of the oil capitals of the world, and to change the face of the industry in the West. Cullinan grasped the significance of Glenn Pool as quickly as any one, and, as at Sour Lake, he was the first to act. The importance of his action on Texaco history has been incalculable. As already noted, Oklahoma crude (the Indian Territory became a part of Oklahoma in 1907) was vastly superior, for the products then made, to the crude previously available. It made such excellent gasoline and kerosine that refineries, not in Texas alone but elsewhere, could profit by using Oklahoma crude for fine processing and other crude for fuel oils. The drawback was transportation. It cost 78 cents a barrel to move oil in tank cars from Tulsa to Port Arthur. That was more than the oil was worth in Tulsa. Yet, so useful was the product to refiners that trains of tank cars rumbled southward day and night.

The Texas Company determined upon another audacious stroke. It would connect the Indian Territory with the Gulf by extending its Port Arthur-to-Humble pipe line with an eight-inch line all the way to Tulsa, although the Glenn Pool crude would be the pipe line's only supply. The cost would be somewhere between $4,000,000 and $10,000,000. When proposed in September, 1906, the total assets of The Texas Company were just under $8,000,000. But the year's profits were nearly a million, and dividends aggregated $609,000. The shareholders voted October 17 to raise $6,000,000 on a fresh issue of Texaco stock. Thirty days later, surveying crews were laying out the route, and within a hundred days dirt was flying. The line, 473 miles long, was finished in a little more than a year, at a cost of $5,641,000. Before it was entirely completed, a portion of it brought Oklahoma crude to North Texas as early as November, 1907. It carried crude for the use of The Texas Company and for competitors. The line was a money-maker from the start.

Texaco was well equipped otherwise to move oil. By 1910, it had 1,010 tank cars, an ocean-going fleet of five tankers, and 19 barges. It had its Amesville, Louisiana, terminal, and a similar terminal at Marcus Hook, Pennsylvania, on the Delaware River, established in 1906. Also, it had terminals at Bayonne, New Jersey; Baltimore, Maryland; and Providence, Rhode Island, as well as the original Port Arthur terminal built in 1902. The forward position of the Company in the matter of waterborne transportation was a factor in its early conquest of foreign markets. W. A. Thompson, Jr., head of the Marine Department, was emerging as one of the Company's strong men.

Another of Cullinan's "boys," as he called them, fast coming to the front, was Ralph C. Holmes, head of the Refining Department. Holmes was one of the ablest men in his field in the country. Nothing short of the best in the way of products satisfied him. He early sensed the future of automobile gasoline, and he set out to make the maximum gasoline from a barrel of crude oil.

The growing Company moved its headquarters from Beaumont to Houston in 1908, establishing general offices in the Stewart Building. In 1914, construction was begun on Texaco's own 13-story building. By 1910, the Company had added three refineries to its original one at Port Arthur. They were at Port Neches, West Tulsa, and West Dallas. In 1911, the fifth refinery was built at Lockport, Illinois, just outside Chicago. In 1913, the assets of the Company passed the $60,000,000 mark. Its capital amounted to $30,000,000, represented by 300,000 shares of $100 value outstanding—this as against $3,000,000 capital and 30,000 shares 10 years before. The increases in capital had been necessary to finance Cullinan's program of unceasing expansion—for instance, the Tulsa-to-Gulf pipe line. More than that, the Company had borrowed money, represented by bonds and notes aggregating $16,400,000. Cullinan demanded that profits and dividends be subordinated to the strengthening of the Company, with an eye to the future.

The young Company was more than making its way against the competition of fellow independents and against Standard. In 1911, all the independents received a hand in their fight against the Standard Oil "trust" from the United States Supreme Court, which dissolved the "trust" as a combination in restraint of trade. In the place of the Standard Oil Company of New Jersey and its 37 subsidiary companies, 38 independent companies were created.

4. The Pioneer's Task Is Ended

*An era ends when Cullinan, the man who
had perhaps done more than any other
to create The Texas Company, leaves in 1913*

The year 1913 witnessed the end of the pioneering period of The Texas Company. At the same time, it saw the departure of the man who had done as much as, and perhaps more than, any other to create that company—J. S. Cullinan. Under Cullinan, Texaco had more and more become a one-man show. The man who had struck out on his own rather than work for anybody else apparently was insisting that his policies be followed, and on being the boss of whatever he had to do with. Some of the other influential stockholders determined upon courses different from his own, and the Executive Committee did not always accede to his wishes. So, when Cullinan could no longer be boss of everything that went on in Texaco, he resigned. He formed another company and remained a considerable figure in the southwestern oil industry, but thereafter he never achieved the success that had been his with The Texas Company.

The situation had been building up for some years. In the beginning, three groups had supplied the capital with which Cullinan started Texaco—Cullinan and the Hogg-Swayne group of Texans; Schlaet and the Laphams from New York; Gates and fellow capitalists, largely from Chicago.

Although he never served as an elected officer of the Company, Gates maintained an active interest in its affairs. He attended Directors' meetings and toured the oil fields on inspection trips. He watched sales figures and made pointed comments. He worked closely with Cullinan and Schlaet in the early years, and opened many a door in banking and railroad circles that otherwise would have been closed to Texaco. Gates liked Cullinan's nerve and backed his resolute, if sometimes risky, program of expansion. Schlaet was more cautious. He would have gone slower. He would have spent less money. His letters to the Laphams began to fill with complaints about Cullinan. The Company should "abstain from having a look at everything that comes along," he wrote. Differences also took on a sectional twist. The New York offices, over which Schlaet presided, had grown to respectable proportions. But the seat of authority was with Cullinan, wherever he was, and he was mostly in Texas. Schlaet complained that Cullinan treated the New York headquarters as "the tail of the dog."

It is a fact that Cullinan was rarely in the New York offices. For that matter, he did not spend a great deal of time in his office in Houston. He ran the Company from the field, where the work was going on. But an excellent office man was rising in the Company. He was Elgood C. Lufkin, an Easterner, and a graduate of Massachusetts Institute of Technology, who, after a successful career as a manufacturer of heavy machinery, had been hired to manage Texaco's natural gas properties. Quickly he became a Vice President, where his affable manners, diplomacy, and skill at administration were useful to a company headed by a rough-and-tumble pioneer like Cullinan. In 1911, Lufkin moved his office to New York.

The deaths of Gates and Gates' son, who was also a Director, weakened Cullinan's position. In 1913, he lost control of the Executive Committee of the Board. That spelled the end of one-man rule of Texaco. On November 25, 1913, Cullinan left The Texas Company and the Directors chose E. C. Lufkin as President.

So ended an era.

II.

1914-1933

The
Gasoline Era

Elgood C. Lufkin

Elgood Chauncey Lufkin was born in Springfield, Massachusetts, February 5, 1864. In 1869, he went to Titusville, Pennsylvania, with his father, who was an oilman. He was graduated from Massachusetts Institute of Technology in 1886 as a mechanical engineer, worked with a pipe line company for several years, and was general manager of the Snow Steam Pump Works in Buffalo from 1895 to 1909. He joined Texaco at Houston in 1909 as Manager of the Natural Gas Department, and on November 16, 1909, was made a Director and Vice President. On November 25, 1913, he was elected President, and on March 23, 1920, Chairman of the Board. On March 9, 1926, he resigned as Chairman, but continued as a Director until April 28, 1931. Mr. Lufkin died at Rye, New York, October 9, 1935.

Amos L. Beaty

Amos Leonidas Beaty was born in Red River County, Texas, September 1, 1870. He studied law, and in 1891 was admitted to the bar. The next year he became a member of the firm of Wilkins & Beaty at Sherman, Texas. He joined The Texas Company at Dallas in 1907 as a member of the legal staff. Three years later he was transferred to Houston where, in 1911, he was appointed Associate General Attorney. In 1913, he was transferred to New York, and on November 25, 1913, was elected General Counsel and a Director. "Judge" Beaty, who had served as general counsel of Producers Oil Company and as president of Texas Petroleum Company, was elected Texaco's President March 23, 1920, and Chairman March 16, 1926. He resigned December 21, 1927. On April 29, 1939, he died in New York City.

Ralph C. Holmes

Ralph Clinton Holmes was born August 24, 1874, at Sharon Center, Pennsylvania. His high school education was obtained at Olean, New York, and he spent part of his vacation time in his home town learning the oil business. He was employed by the Standard Oil Company for several years. He joined The Texas Company in May, 1902, and became Superintendent of the Refining Department, later Manager of the department. He became a Director May 29, 1906, and a Vice President January 6, 1913. He held presidencies and directorships in several Texaco subsidiaries and was elected President of The Texas Company March 16, 1926. He became Chairman of the Board of Directors April 25, 1933, and resigned May 5, 1933. Mr. Holmes died December 23, 1950, in Orlando, Florida.

5. New Methods
Create New Markets

Texaco's policy of concentrating
on automobile fuel pays off. The Company quadruples in size
and gets the Holmes-Manley thermal cracking process

By 1914, changes which were bound to have far-reaching effects on the Company's future development were beginning to take shape. World War I brought an immense increase in the demand for petroleum products. Then the automobile became a necessity in modern American life, and the gasoline market expanded rapidly.

The period from 1914 to 1933 in The Texas Company was marked by steady technical and scientific advances, by spectacular growth in the production and sale of gasoline and lubricating oils, and in refining, transporting, and marketing petroleum products. This period includes the administrations of E. C. Lufkin, Amos L. Beaty, and R. C. Holmes.

Mr. Schlaet relinquished his office as First Vice President in 1914, although he continued as a Director, and as Chairman of the Executive Committee, until the close of 1919.

In the six years from 1914 to the end of 1920, the Company practically quadrupled in assets. This phenomenal growth was due in large part to the tremendous demand for petroleum products resulting from World War I, but was also a result of the remarkable increase in the use of the automobile. The Texas Company made a specialty of automobile gasoline and lubricating oils. It laid the foundation for leadership in service to the motorist that to this day remains unsurpassed.

The early part of this period also witnessed the further

THE HORSE WAS PUT TO PASTURE

AND OIL-POWERED TANK TRUCKS TOOK OVER

ANOTHER NEW BULK PLANT MARKED TEXACO'S ENTRY INTO MANITOU SPRINGS, COLORADO

development of The Texas Company as an integrated oil company—the course on which it embarked when it was founded. When World War I created a shortage in tankers and it was impossible to buy them, William A. Thompson, Jr., of the Marine Department leased a yard in Maine to keep Texaco's growing tanker fleet up to the needs of the expanding business. The Company discovered its own clay and fuller's earth beds, so as to be independent of suppliers of these materials essential to refining. It made its own oil cans. It acquired timberlands and a sawmill to produce lumber for its packing cases. For a while, it made its own tank wagons.

When World War I started, in 1914, The Texas Company sustained its first war loss within a matter of days when the Belgians burned the Texaco installations at Antwerp to keep them from the invading Germans. Later, the Texaco tanker *Illinois* was torpedoed and sunk in the English Channel. Of Texaco's 14,000 employes in the United States, 2,986 entered the service.

As Vice President for two years and, later, as President, Mr. Lufkin maintained his office in New York, although Texaco was still a Texas corporation. The corporate laws of the State of Texas reflected a feeling prevalent in many parts of the West at that time. This was distrust of great corporations, particularly multiple corporations operating in many states. The Texas Company was organized under a statute which authorized the creation of corporations for storing, transporting, buying, and selling oil and gas *in that state*. Almost immediately after its organization, The Texas Company was doing business in other states, and it was also refining oil in Texas—activities which came under the implied rather than the stated powers of its charter.

The Company, under the guidance of its General Counsel, Amos L. Beaty, undertook to remove the possibility of a misunderstanding with the state authorities. It was in 1915 that the Texas Legislature passed a measure, popularly known as the Texas Company Bill, which gave oil companies permission to engage, both within and without the State of Texas, in all phases of oil operations, except producing. In 1917, permission to engage in oil and gas production was added to the list, and the Producers Oil Company, by then a subsidiary, was absorbed by the parent corporation. This legislation was a compliment to The Texas Company that speaks well for its record in Texas.

We have mentioned how Texaco anticipated the increased use of gasoline. It was a fortunate anticipation. The growth of the automotive industry was the wonder of the age. In 1919, there were 8,132,000 passenger cars registered in the United States, a nine-fold increase since 1912. There were 1,108,000 trucks, a 27-fold increase. World War I demonstrated the effectiveness of the truck over the Army mule. By 1919, the automotive industry, coming up from nothing in 20 years, was almost as large, in assets, as the petroleum industry, and within a few years it was to be larger. The rise of aviation during the war also spurred the demand for gasoline. So it was that, about 1915, the production of gasoline in the United States as a whole passed that of kerosine, until then the mainstay of the industry. In The Texas Company, this pivotal change had taken place earlier.

At home and abroad, Texaco's selling efforts were extended greatly. No other oil company, certainly no small company, advertised so widely. The red star with the green "T" was emblazoned on all the Company's property that was visible to the public. Retailers displayed it. Newspaper and magazine ads called attention to the virtues of "Texaco Gasoline—More Miles per Gallon" and "Texaco Motor Oil—The Care Free Oil." By 1915, The Texas Company was selling more motor gasoline than its refineries could produce. The deficit was made up by purchases from other refiners.

One of the incidental by-products of that advertising is worthy of note. It was read by a young mining engineer in California named Rodgers, who reflected that The Texas Company must be a live outfit. William Starling Sullivant Rodgers, a graduate of Sheffield Scientific School at Yale, was working for the small American Oriental Oil Company at Martinez. In 1915, he joined Texaco's Refining Department and was assigned to the laboratory of the asphalt plant at Port Neches, Texas. If the

Company's 1915 advertising appropriation did nothing more than get the services of Rodgers, it was money well spent.

It did a good deal more, though. It helped boost motor gasoline sales, and the management soon realized that it would be necessary to produce more gasoline from every barrel of crude oil.

Prior to 1914, several scientists in the country were working on thermal cracking processes to obtain a larger yield of gasoline from a barrel of crude oil. Among them were Joseph H. Adams, the Cross brothers in Kansas City, C. P. Dubbs, Dr. W. M. Burton (who later became president of the Standard Oil Company of Indiana), and others. The Burton process, developed by Dr. Burton and placed in operation by Indiana Standard in 1913, was the first of the thermal cracking processes widely used in commercial operation.

Using the Burton process, the Indiana company and some of the other companies licensed to use it were obtaining a much higher gasoline yield than The Texas Company's Refining Department was able to get. Should this disturbing trend continue, Texaco's gasoline profits would go out the window, or the Company would have to buy a license from Standard of Indiana.

The Burton process had the disadvantage of being a batch process, in which the equipment operated only about one-half the time, and its yields of gasoline were comparatively low. A continuous process with higher yields was the goal on which Texaco set its sights. The problem was tackled in New York and Texas.

In New York, Mr. Lufkin and others made arrangements with Joseph H. Adams for The Texas Company to take over his liquid-phase patents on a new cracking process. They also obtained patents from William A. Hall on a vapor-phase process, which was worked on at Bayonne, New Jersey.

In Port Arthur, R. C. Holmes, head of the Refining Department, and Fred T. Manley, assisted by Dr. G. W. Gray, Otto Behimer, and others, also were working on the problem of thermal cracking.

Ralph Holmes was a self-educated man operating in a highly technical field that was rapidly being dominated by products of the scientific schools. After finishing high school, he had gone to work for Standard in Pennsylvania. In 1902, Cullinan brought him to Port Arthur to help erect Texaco's first refinery. Within a few years, he was in charge of the department.

Like Mr. Holmes, Fred Manley had never set foot inside a college. He had gone to work in the Pennsylvania oil fields as a boy, and had joined The Texas Company as a laborer in 1902. He was soon promoted to be engineer of the fondly remembered *Texas Girl*.

Ultimately, the Holmes-Manley process, based on the Adams patents, was perfected. It was put into operation in 1920. This was the first continuous thermal cracking process that was both practical and commercially profitable. The early purchase of the Adams inventions, the development by The Texas Company of the so-called "clean circulation" principle involved in the Holmes-Manley process, and the ownership of the Behimer patents covering it, put Texaco in a very strong position. The Company was able to acquire a valuable patent and process position in the cracking field and issued licenses generally to the industry. Once again, as a result of these developments, it forged ahead; this time, because of the percentage of gasoline it could produce from a barrel of crude.

Technical advances were also being made in developing processes for making better lubricating oils and greases. The growing demand for automotive oils brought about a condition The Texas Company could capitalize on, but it was another uphill battle. Most of the oils then used in automobile crankcases were made from Pennsylvania crudes, and were comparatively dark in color. Texaco oils, made from South Texas and South Louisiana crudes, were lighter in color, but they were excellent oils. Nevertheless, the public preference at the time was for the darker oils. Texaco, therefore, made a virtue of necessity by advertising "Texaco Motor Oils—Clean, Clear, Golden," and by displaying them in glass bottles at service stations. The Company's production of lubricating oils rose from 266,000 barrels in 1914 to 1,511,000 in 1920.

In developing the market for Texaco gasoline and lubricating oils, the Company deliberately sacrificed the commanding position it had held as one of the early marketers of fuel oil in quantity. This concentration on the needs of the automobile and the truck was a matter of policy, and it paid big dividends. Even today, Texaco is not a comparatively large producer of fuel oils and furnace oils.

New producing fields that were opened at Breckenridge and Burkburnett in northern Texas, at West Columbia on the Texas Gulf Coast, in the Texas Panhandle, and in Oklahoma and Kansas increased The Texas Company's crude production, but these increases did not keep Texaco abreast of what the industry as a whole was doing.

During this period of expansion in refinery facilities, including cracking equipment, in the 1920's, gasoline production and sales forged ahead, but The Texas Company's percentage of production to the total crude oil production in the United States (which had reached a peak of 7.03 per cent in 1915) declined to a low of 2.48 per cent in 1924. Then, when the California Petroleum Corporation was acquired in 1928, the percentage position improved again. In 1933, when producing conditions were becoming less chaotic, Texaco's production was 4.06 per cent of the United States total. It has maintained or bettered this position ever since.

Old rule-of-thumb methods were giving way to the scientific approach. The studies of geologists reduced the number of dry holes that The Texas Company put down. Despite the head-shaking and even the ridicule of old-timers, C. N. Scott, Vice President in charge of production, started a training program to instruct young college graduates in the art of drilling wells. Scott's school was successful, and a forerunner of the petroleum engineering courses now conducted in colleges. Unfortunately, however, Mr. Scott did not have the complete backing of the Directors. Although he gathered together a small nucleus of scientists, money was not forthcoming to maintain the Company's position, as to production, in the industry.

THE COMPANY'S FIRST REFINERY, AT PORT ARTHUR, TEXAS, LOOKED LIKE THIS BACK IN 1903

IN THE 1920'S, THESE REVOLUTIONARY HOLMES-MANLEY STILLS CHANGED THE PICTURE

NOW, PORT ARTHUR WORKS PROCESSES PETROLEUM AT A DAILY RATE OF 200,000 BARRELS

The number of stockholders increased from 1,453 in 1914 to 11,821 in 1920. In part, this was due to increased employe participation in the Company's ownership. Employes were permitted to buy stock and pay for it in installments. The Company also introduced a system of death and disability benefits for employes. The dividend policy continued to be conservative. A large part of the earnings was plowed back into the business.

Early in 1920, there was a change in the top management. The office of Chairman of the Board was created, and Mr. Lufkin resigned the presidency to fill it. Judge Beaty, the General Counsel, was elected President.

6. Serving the Motorist

The 1920's find Texaco producing, refining, and marketing
the country over. Gasoline sales increase,
and "service station" becomes part of the language

Between 1920 and 1926, The Texas Company stepped up its activities in the Rocky Mountain region. Consequently, with the exception of the Pacific Coast, the Company was refining and marketing in every geographical division of the United States.

Refinery problems received the most attention. Although other products were not neglected (the Company's Port Neches, Texas, refinery was by then the largest asphalt plant in the world), the emphasis during this period was on the manufacture and sale of gasoline and lubricating oils. At the end of 1920, The Texas Company was turning only 20.99 per cent of a barrel of crude into gasoline, whereas the industry as a whole converted

26.1 per cent. By 1923, Texaco's average was 33.8 per cent to 30 per cent for the industry. In 1924, President Beaty noted that gasoline manufacture increased 43 per cent over that of 1923. In 1925, with more Holmes-Manley cracking units in operation, Texaco was able to refine into gasoline 44.2 per cent of a barrel of crude. The industry figure was 32.4 per cent.

In 1925, Texaco manufactured 15,213,000 barrels of motor fuel, against 6,595,000 in 1920. This brought refinery output abreast of sales for the first time since 1917.

In the year 1926, The Texas Company introduced Texaco New and Better Gasoline. The quality of this product far surpassed that of any competitive gasoline then available.

By 1927, Texaco's sales of lubricating oil reached almost 62,665,000 gallons. The Company was making and selling nearly six times as much oil as in 1914.

This constitutes a fine tribute to the Texaco sales organization. C. P. Dodge, who was Secretary of the Company, and C. E. Woodbridge, who was later elected Treasurer, for many years were the active heads of the sales organizations in the South and North, respectively. W. A. Thompson, Jr., a Vice President after 1913, had general supervision of sales, particularly in foreign fields. Much of the impetus toward greater sales came from them.

By 1926, Texaco could point to the fact that its products were sold in 46 states—a record unequaled by any competitor. To be sure, 56 per cent of the Company's sales were in eight states: Texas, New York, Florida, North Carolina, Illinois, Virginia, New Jersey, and Pennsylvania. The strengthening of the Company's position in other regions was work for the future.

In the 1920's, the number of domestic retail outlets where Texaco gasoline was sold increased substantially. By 1927, in addition to the thousands of independent retail outlets in the United States that sold Texaco products, Texaco either owned, or leased, more than 4,000 stations. At about this time, the Texaco people began to substitute the term "service station" for "filling station."

There were large gains abroad. The Company enlarged its

share of the European market. Sales also increased in Latin America and in Africa. The Company went into New Zealand and the Philippines.

By this time, Texaco was making full use of scientific advances. Such scientific developments not only helped the Company directly. They gave it something to trade with other companies in the industry. Better products for the public, more economical operation of the Company's plants, and patent revenue for the benefit of Texaco stockholders resulted from cross-licensing arrangements (which made possible the use of patent rights of other companies) and from licensing Texaco's own patent rights to others.

The financial prosperity of the Company continued. The expansion of the business was financed from earnings, and from the proceeds of new issues of capital stock which were eagerly taken.

These shares were more widely distributed among individual owners. In 1921, dividends went on a $3-a-share basis, and remained there until the depression year of 1931.

In March, 1926, President Beaty succeeded E. C. Lufkin as Chairman of the Board, and R. C. Holmes was elected to the presidency of the Company. Mr. Lufkin continued as a Director until 1931.

The accomplishments from 1914 down to the middle 1920's were no longer the doings of one or two men, as had been the case in the Company's earlier years. The organization had grown too big for that. The management group was larger, and most of its members had their roots far back in the Company's beginnings. These Company leaders did not always agree on minor, or, for that matter, on major matters. Personal rivalries often loomed large, and sectional differences sometimes caused them to line up against one another. But all had achieved a background of experience that enabled them to see the Company's complete picture right back to the beginnings, and to recognize the larger objectives, no matter what might be the difficulties of the moment.

7. The Feast and the Famine

Texaco takes over three other companies,
increases domestic production,
and then, in 1931, sustains an operating loss

The years from 1926 to 1931 were also ones of great expansion. The Company's pipe line systems were extended into new areas, refineries were built or acquired at Amarillo, San Antonio, and El Paso, Texas; Cody and La Barge, Wyoming; Sunburst, Montana; Craig, Colorado; and Los Angeles and Fillmore, California. Sales were also expanded to include all the states of the Union and numerous towns and cities where Texaco heretofore had not marketed. The three years that followed witnessed a reversal of this trend, and a period of retrenchment was necessary, as The Texas Company, in common with industry generally, fought the great depression.

A number of men advanced to positions of greater responsibility. W. S. S. Rodgers, by then General Superintendent of Terminals, was given special duties in the Executive Offices beginning the latter part of 1925. His principal assignment was to arrange for the sale of licenses for Holmes-Manley cracking stills to other refiners. In April, 1926, he was promoted to Assistant to the President. He was promoted because he had made it his business to study the operations of the Company as a whole. His duties at the head office afforded an unrivaled opportunity to continue that study. One of his early jobs had to do with sales. He was presently advanced to Vice President in charge of domestic sales, in 1928.

Another new Vice President was Torkild Rieber, a colorful

as well as forceful figure. Born in Norway, Rieber had gone to sea as a boy in a sailing ship. He was the 19-year-old mate of one of the first tankers to load oil at Port Arthur after the Spindletop strike in 1901. Four years later, The Texas Company bought the tanker of which Rieber was then chief officer. Thereafter, "Cap" Rieber's periodical sojourns ashore at Port Arthur were remembered events. The genial seaman, with a seaman's salty language and a ready smile, was easy to know and easy to like. Before long, The Texas Company employed him ashore, in the Marine and Refining Departments. In 1919, he left to join J. S. Cullinan, and later became president of the Galena-Signal Oil Company, a Cullinan enterprise. In 1927, Rieber returned to Texaco, to head the Export Department and, later, the Marine Department as well.

Still another Company officer to gain stature during this period was Harry T. Klein, the General Counsel. Col. Klein had come to The Texas Company as a consequence of his service in the Army. Our entry into World War I found Klein practicing law in Cincinnati, across the Ohio River from his native Kentucky. Enlisting as a private, he was commissioned a second lieutenant of infantry, but after his arrival in France he was transferred to the Judge Advocate General's department. He finished the war a lieutenant colonel and the Chief Requisitions Officer of the American Expeditionary Forces. Among other honors, he was awarded a Distinguished Service Medal. After the Armistice, Edwin B. Parker, a Houston lawyer, went to France to represent the United States in damage claims arising from the war. Parker induced Col. Klein to remain abroad until 1920, attending to such matters. When Klein returned home, Parker was General Counsel of The Texas Company. He got Klein to join the staff, and in 1925, Klein himself became General Counsel.

At about this time, Judge Beaty and the Company's lawyers were busy with the details of a reorganization of Texaco's corporate structure. Under the corporation laws of Texas, it was difficult to achieve the flexibility needed for a necessarily com-

MODERN TEXACO DEALER SERVICE STATIONS ARE NOW FAMILIAR SIGHTS IN ALL 48 STATES

BY THE 1920'S, TEXACO HAD BECOME A FAVORITE SUPPLIER OF THE MOTORIST'S NEEDS

plex enterprise doing business over most of the world. Consequently, the legal home of the Company was transferred to Delaware, although the actual headquarters remained in New York. The bulk of the Company's producing and refining operations still took place in Texas and bordering states, because that was where the oil was. Despite the great geographical expansion of the Company's operations since then, this remains substantially the case today.

The basic corporate changes were brought about in this way: The Texas *Corporation* was organized in 1926 under the laws of Delaware and by exchange of shares acquired substantially all the outstanding stock of The Texas Company (of Texas). In 1927, the entire assets of the latter company were transferred to, and its officers and personnel were taken over by, a newly formed Delaware corporation named The Texas *Company*, a subsidiary of The Texas *Corporation*, and The Texas Company (of Texas) was dissolved. The Texas *Company* (of Delaware) assigned to its parent the shares of 19 companies which had been acquired in the above mentioned transfer of assets. (The italics are the writer's.)

By these steps The Texas Corporation was established as a holding company, with The Texas Company (of Delaware) as its principal operating subsidiary. This situation continued until 1941, when further corporate changes were made. Although, when referring to the over-all operations of the Texaco enterprise during the period 1927 to 1941, it would be technically correct to speak of The Texas Corporation and its subsidiaries, the writer, for the sake of simplicity, is going to stick to the name "The Texas Company" straight through.

Effective November 1, 1941, The Texas Corporation underwent a reorganization by which The Texas Corporation merged into itself The Texas Company (Delaware) and caused The Texas Company (California) to be dissolved. The Texas Corporation, as of November 1, 1941, acquired all of the assets and assumed all of the liabilities of both these companies, and thereafter became known as The Texas Company.

Considerable of The Texas Company's large-scale expansion in the late '20's was due to the taking over of the California Petroleum Corporation, in 1928; the Galena-Signal Oil Company, in the same year; and, in 1931, the Indian Refining Company, operating in the Middle West. These transactions, involving $104,000,000 in assets, could have been swung only by a prosperous company. The new facilities could have been merged smoothly with the Texaco organization only by a company that knew what it wanted and where it was going.

The acquisition of California Petroleum, later to be The Texas Company (California), spread the red star with the green "T" over the Pacific slope. Overnight, the Texaco emblem blossomed on service stations, tank trucks, refineries, terminals, and all the facilities of the former California Petroleum Corporation. Even before the California deal, The Texas Company operated the largest number of refineries of any American oil company. These plants were also the most widely distributed, being located in 10 states, from Rhode Island to Wyoming. Now, Texaco had five others, with a daily capacity of 42,000 barrels of crude—three of them in California, one in Montana, and one in Wyoming. From the California company, Texaco also obtained producing wells, casing-head gasoline plants, pipe lines, tankers, ocean terminals, and extensive marketing facilities throughout the western states.

Galena-Signal was not the large or the thriving organization that California Petroleum was. Yet it had facilities that The Texas Company could use. There was a 20,000-barrel refinery at Houston, some tankage, tank ships, two deep-water terminals, and foreign marketing subsidiaries.

By acquiring control of the Indian Refining Company, Texaco also acquired important dewaxing patents which were used in the processing of premium motor oils. It was the cost of developing solvent dewaxing, coupled with the depression, that put Indian in a position where it was willing to sell to Texaco. At one time, this company had done business in 24 states. With the onset of hard times, it pulled out of the gasoline market in all but five—eastern Illinois, Indiana, western Ohio, Kentucky, and Michigan. Indian did 20 per cent of the gasoline business in Indiana. Its distribution and sales machinery in the five states was quite complete and an important addition to Texaco.

Texaco continued to keep itself in the public eye. Capt. Frank M. Hawks, Superintendent of the Company's Aviation Division, was promoting the cause of aviation by a series of record-breaking speed flights in Texaco aircraft, including the famous *Texaco No. 13*.

Emphasis was being placed on refining in the 1920's by The Texas Company and some other large companies. Since the advent of cracking, the refining end of the business had been the most profitable of all. There were still other companies, on the contrary, that while not neglecting refining were emphasizing crude oil production and the building up of reserves. The Directors of The Texas Company felt that proven crude oil production could be bought for less than the cost to the Company for exploration and development. This view continued to be held even when most other companies rushed into the booming East Texas field late in 1930, and resulted in Texaco's occupying a relatively minor position there as compared with its competitors.

The Company's 1929 earnings were the largest up to that time, but before the end of the year the stock market collapsed. The discovery of East Texas in the Fall of 1930, combined with the depression of the early '30's, reversed the earnings picture of the entire industry and of The Texas Company.

By 1931, The Texas Company was losing money. It continued to pay dividends to the stockholders, but on a reduced basis.

To offset the effects of the depression, The Texas Company brought out Texaco Fire Chief Gasoline in 1932. There was some opposition to the launching of a new product when everything seemed to be at the bottom. The proponents of the new product argued that something was needed to halt the decline in gasoline sales, both for the sake of the Company and its dealers, some of whom were going out of business. Their argument won, and Texaco Fire Chief Gasoline was introduced with a fanfare of advertising, including a full-scale comedy radio program on a nationwide hookup. Ed Wynn, a top-ranking comedian, was the star, and it was the first large radio show to raise the glass curtain between audience and performers and broadcast before a "live" audience.

In the same year, Texaco began to promote its automobile chassis lubricant, Marfak, on a wider scale. Marfak is from the Arabic, a name for one of the stars. Even before the Company adopted the red star with the green "T" as its trade mark, Texaco's advertising men had christened Texaco products with the names of heavenly bodies. This custom of naming many Texaco products has been carried along to the present day, notably in the Ursa, Crater, Algol, and Aries series of Texaco lubricants.

Company-wide, the dollar losses of 1931 were cut by nearly four-fifths in 1932, but it was apparent that further improvements could and should be made. At the Directors' meeting of April 25, 1933, R. C. Holmes was elected Chairman of the Board and W. S. S. Rodgers became President. On May 5, Mr. Holmes resigned the chairmanship, and was succeeded by Charles B. Ames. Judge Ames, a former Director and Vice President of the Company in charge of the Legal Department, had resigned in November, 1932, to become president of the American Petroleum Institute.

CAPT. HAWKS WAS A RECORD BREAKER

III.

1934-1952

The Era
of Conservation

MODERN CONSERVATION OF OIL RESERVES BEGINS WITH PLANNED SPACING OF WELLS

8. Taking the Long View

Management, not satisfied with crude production and
underground reserves, determines that the Company no longer
will rely on the purchase of proven production

The outlook for The Texas Company was anything but rosy when the new management team stepped in. Due to the depression and overproduction in East Texas, prices for products in the first half of 1933 were at an all-time low. Consequently, the Company was still operating in the red, and morale, too, was low.

To look at him, William Starling Sullivant Rodgers, the new President, had the appearance of a good man in a situation of this kind. Forty-seven years old when he took the presidency, Rodgers was a tall, strongly built man with an air of confidence and calmness about him that inspired subordinates to confidence in themselves. He looked the fact that he had spent much of his life out-of-doors. When he spoke, he spoke deliberately, and his tone was one of assurance.

Conditions began to improve in the country and in the petroleum industry in the latter part of 1933. Texaco's loss for the year was $491,004, the last loss on a year's operations the Company has sustained to date.

Until the oil boom in East Texas in 1930, the oil industry had gone through alternating periods of feast and famine; first overproduction, then shortages of crude oil. The East Texas field focused public attention on the choice between true conservation or reckless waste of an irreplaceable natural resource. The State of Texas recognized the problem and undertook to do something

Charles B. Ames

W. S. S. Rodgers

Charles Bismark Ames was born in Macon, Mississippi, August 1, 1870. He was educated at Emory and Henry College and the University of Mississippi. He practiced law in his home town and in Oklahoma City, served as a Supreme Court judge in Oklahoma, did important state and Federal work during World War I, and in 1919 was appointed an Assistant to the Attorney General of the United States. He came to The Texas Company in 1923, and on March 27 was elected General Counsel as well as a Director. He left The Texas Company on December 28, 1925, and returned January 18, 1928, as a Director and Vice President. He held these two positions until November 22, 1932, when he again resigned to head the American Petroleum Institute. On May 5, 1933, he was recalled to Texaco to become Chairman of the Board, and held that office until his death in Meredith, New Hampshire, July 21, 1935. During his service with The Texas Company, Judge Ames held directorships in California Petroleum Corporation, The Texas Company (California), Seaboard Oil Company of Delaware, and Indian Refining Company.

William Starling Sullivant Rodgers was born February 19, 1886, in Columbus, Ohio. Following his graduation from the Sheffield Scientific School of Yale University, he entered upon a mining career in the West and, later, served in oil companies on the Pacific Coast. He joined Texaco on November 1, 1915, at Port Neches, Texas, where he worked in the laboratory and on stills and converters. He served in World War I and attained the rank of captain in the Ordnance Department. After his return to Texaco he advanced through various foremanships and superintendencies and on April 20, 1926, was named Assistant to the President, Executive Offices, New York. He became a Vice President October 1, 1928, and a Director November 27, 1928. On April 25, 1933, he was elected President, and became chief executive officer August 9, 1935. On April 25, 1944, Mr. Rodgers became Chairman of the Board. Over the years, he has held chairmanships, presidencies, and directorships in many of Texaco's subsidiary and affiliated companies. He is a former chairman of Arabian American Oil Company and Trans-Arabian Pipe Line Company.

Torkild Rieber

Harry T. Klein

Torkild Rieber was born in Bergen, Norway, March 13, 1882. He went to sea on a sailing vessel at the age of 13, was graduated from nautical academies abroad, served as an officer on sailing vessels and steamships all over the world, and passed his examination for master in New York City. He was mate of one of the first tankers to load crude oil from the Spindletop field. He joined Texaco in July, 1905, as chief officer on an oil tanker, served the Marine and Refining Departments in various capacities, left Texaco in 1919 to join J. S. Cullinan, and later became president of the Galena-Signal Oil Company, a Cullinan enterprise. In 1927, he returned to take charge of Texaco's foreign operations and Marine Department. He became a Vice President March 20, 1928, and a Director November 27, 1928. He was elected Chairman of the Board August 9, 1935, and resigned as such August 12, 1940, and as a Director August 23, 1940. "Cap" Rieber held chairmanships, presidencies, and directorships in many of The Texas Company's subsidiaries and affiliated companies, the majority of which operated in foreign countries.

Harry Thomas Klein was born in Bellevue, Kentucky, March 22, 1886. He attended public schools there, and was graduated from the McDonald Institute at Cincinnati, Ohio, with a law degree. For some years he taught and practiced law in Cincinnati. He served overseas in World War I, becoming lieutenant colonel judge advocate, and at the end of the war was special counsel to the United States Liquidation Commission in France. He joined The Texas Company May 1, 1921, as Assistant General Counsel in the Legal Department, New York. He became General Counsel in 1925, Vice President and General Counsel, as well as a Director, in 1933, and Executive Vice President in 1940. He was elected President April 25, 1944. On April 22, 1952, he was elected Chairman of the Executive Committee. Col. Klein has served as a director of a number of The Texas Company's principal subsidiary and affiliated companies, including Texaco Development Corporation, Arabian American Oil Company, McColl-Frontenac Oil Company Limited, Jefferson Chemical Company, Inc., and Trans-Arabian Pipe Line Company.

about it. Governor Ross Sterling of Texas and many oil industry leaders, and other businessmen, took the lead in sponsoring adequate state legislation to bring about the conservation of crude oil. By 1935, there were effective conservation laws on the statute books of the States of Texas, Louisiana, Oklahoma, and other oil-producing states. In Texas, the Texas Railroad Commission under the leadership of Col. (later Lt. Gen.) Ernest O. Thompson was the enforcing agency. The Federal Government backed up such state laws with the Connally Hot Oil Act, which prohibited the transportation of illegally produced oil from one state to another.

Moreover, in 1935, certain of the leading oil producing states, with the consent of Congress, entered into an interstate compact the purpose of which was to encourage the conservation of oil and gas by the prevention of physical waste. Each member state agreed to enact a conservation statute, or, if it already had one, to continue it in effect. A commission created by the compact was given certain fact-finding and advisory powers. The compact has been from time to time continued and today, with few exceptions, the principal producing states are members of the Interstate Oil Compact Commission.

Under these laws, the producing life and ultimate recovery of oil fields have been tremendously increased, and it has been possible for the industry to make long-range plans with an assured source of future supply. The way was opened for great expansion and increase in the use of petroleum and its products. The conservation of oil and gas has been a vital factor in stabilizing the oil industry, and was instrumental in building up the reserve producing capacity which was to enable this nation to defend itself from military aggression in World War II.

Early in 1933, The Texas Company was producing about 55 per cent of the crude oil it refined, including royalty oil. It stood fourth or fifth among American oil companies in underground crude reserves, as nearly as it could be reckoned. Yet Texaco's refinery runs were either second or third in this country, and it stood about second in the manufacture and sale of gasoline.

The crude production and underground crude reserve situation did not satisfy Texaco's management, which was now taking a long view of the future and was banking on the conservation laws becoming increasingly effective. The management wanted Texaco to produce enough crude so that its ratio of crude production to refinery runs would be greatly increased. It was determined that the Company would try to find its own crude reserves rather than to rely on the purchase of proven production.

Year by year, the appropriations for the Domestic Producing Department were increased. More and more leases on oil and gas acreage were acquired. In 1933, such holdings amounted to 4,961,000 acres. In 1944, holdings were 10,490,000 acres, and they stand at about 11,500,000 acres now.

Leasing was made more selective. To get the most for its money, the Company improved and enlarged the technical organization of the Producing Department. The staff of geologists, geophysicists, and research and petroleum engineers was expanded. They were given better equipment to work with, some of it developed in the Texaco laboratories. In 1933, the Company had three seismic exploration crews in the field. In 1935, there were 11, and in 1951, 39. This made possible the selection of acreage on a more scientific basis. By 1940, Texaco had more than doubled its domestic crude oil production over that of 1933. Production has continued to increase at a rate greater than the increase in refinery runs, so that the Company is now producing on a gross basis about three-quarters of the crude it refines.

Since the inauguration of this policy, in 1933, it is estimated that The Texas Company has discovered in the United States alone more than 2,800,000,000 barrels of new reserves, a yearly average of close to 148,000,000 barrels, which is far in excess of the yearly amount of oil the Company has taken from the ground. Any company that is discovering new oil reserves in the ground faster than it is taking oil out is in a sound position as to the production needs of the future. Since 1939, The Texas Company's untouched domestic reserves have been exceeded only by those of one competitor.

TODAY, IN PIPE LINE CONSTRUCTION, MACHINERY IS USED FOR DOPING AND WRAPPING

IN 1923, TEXACO PIPELINERS DID WRAPPING JOBS BY HAND

Another problem concerned lubricating oil. Texaco, it will be recalled, had developed good automotive oils soon after 1912 and kept itself among the leaders in this field while the automobile industry was in the early stages of its growth. But when the trend in automobile manufacture in the late 1920's turned toward higher-compression engines that ran considerably hotter than before, Texaco's brand of motor oil did not stand up as well as motor oils made from Pennsylvania crudes, and the competition from the Pennsylvania grade motor oils had become a serious problem.

Texaco acquired control of the Indian Refining Company in 1931. Indian, as we have mentioned, had patents on a solvent process for dewaxing lubricating oil to an unusually low cold test, thereby providing improved cold-weather starting characteristics. These patents, used in making Havoline Waxfree Motor Oil, were acquired as part of Indian's assets. It was decided to sell Indian's long-established Havoline through Texaco dealers as a premium-grade motor oil. In spite of Havoline's high quality, it still was excelled by the premium-grade Pennsylvania oils in certain respects.

Texaco scientists had been working on a process of solvent extraction, using furfural (a product made from oat hulls) as a solvent for separating undesirable constituents from lubricating oil. They concluded that a truly superior oil could be produced from many types of crude by applying the combination of solvent dewaxing and furfural solvent extraction.

A commercial installation for furfural solvent extraction was made at the Lawrenceville, Illinois, refinery. This plant, together with the solvent dewaxing plant that existed, was used to produce a new Havoline oil which Texaco put on the market nationally in 1934 as a premium motor oil in refinery-sealed cans. The new Havoline was of outstanding quality and gained rapid acceptance. It was not long before the Lawrenceville refinery was unable to keep up with the demand for Havoline, and a solvent dewaxing and solvent refining plant was completed at Port Arthur, Texas, in 1935 to augment the supply. This oil had no superior regardless of crude source, and The Texas Company has been careful to maintain Havoline's superiority by improving it steadily through the years.

Solvent dewaxing and solvent extraction not only made possible an improved Havoline, but in 1936 the Port Arthur refinery began to produce New Texaco Motor Oil, made by the solvent refining processes. This improved product also was well received by motorists.

Texaco's solvent dewaxing and solvent extraction methods for motor oil became so important that they were quickly adopted by the petroleum industry, even by the refiners of Pennsylvania oils, and today substantially all high-quality motor oil is made by this procedure. The major portion of such oils is manufactured throughout the world under license from Texaco.

By the middle '30's, Texaco's retail outlets in the United States numbered more than 40,000. Rapidly, one after another, two widely advertised items brought them new business. The first of these was a hitherto more or less unmentionable topic— the sanitary facilities available to motorists at service stations. No national advertiser had ever tackled this in forthright fashion. Texaco sales forces policed this free service which the best stations gave and, in 1938, the Company advertised Texaco Registered Rest Rooms—"*Clean* Across the Country." The "rest room stop" for tourists came to coincide with a refill of the gasoline tank. Not long afterward, Texaco's competitors began to advertise clean rest rooms, too.

The second item was a new gasoline, Texaco Sky Chief, "for those who want the best." A premium gasoline, it was a fitting sales companion for Havoline Motor Oil.

In 1935, The Texas Company began to buy stock in McColl-Frontenac Oil Company Limited of Canada, and by 1948 acquired sufficient stock to become a majority owner of the Canadian concern. The Texas Company of Canada, Limited, a marketing organization formed in 1928 to do business in western Canada, was absorbed by McColl-Frontenac in 1940. Today, McColl-Frontenac, the third largest petroleum marketer in Canada, manufactures and markets petroleum products throughout Canada almost exclusively under Texaco trade marks. It operates refineries at Montreal and Edmonton, and also has a substantial interest in production in western Canada and, through a subsidiary, on the island of Trinidad.

Judge C. B. Ames, who had been Chairman of the Board since 1933, died on July 21, 1935. He was succeeded as Chairman by Torkild Rieber. It will be recalled that "Cap" Rieber had left The Texas Company in 1919 to join Joseph S. Cullinan's enterprises. He had returned to Texaco in 1927 and, in 1928, had become a Vice President in charge of the Company's foreign operations and Marine Department. W. S. S. Rodgers continued as President and became the Company's chief executive officer.

By 1935, the Company's domestic operations had recovered from the ill effects of the depression to a considerable extent and management could again look to the foreign field for production. Thereafter, a part of The Texas Company's forward-looking program was the reorganization and expansion of its foreign business.

In the late 1920's and early 1930's, prospective oil lands had been acquired in Colombia and Venezuela, but the Company had no foreign production from these areas. It had, however, developed a very substantial sales position in Latin America and the Eastern Hemisphere, but out of necessity had supplied these markets from domestic production. It was becoming obvious that it would be impossible to continue to supply these markets from domestic sources in the future without causing financial losses.

Therefore, the Company stepped up its activities in Colombia and Venezuela. In 1936, it acquired approximately one half of the stock of a company which had the controlling interest in the Barco Concession in Colombia. A pipe line from the remote Barco producing area became necessary. This was a costly undertaking. It was completed in 1939, and Barco crude then began coming on the market.

In 1940, Texaco formed, jointly with Caracas Petroleum,

S.A., a company which acquired from Caracas Petroleum concessions in Venezuela. The search for oil in Venezuela was slowed by World War II, and very little crude was produced there by companies in which Texaco is interested until after the war.

Other prospective oil lands were acquired in Colombia and Venezuela, but the overshadowing foreign development of the period occurred on the other side of the world. In 1936, The Texas Company completed negotiations with the Standard Oil Company of California whereby Texaco's marketing facilities east of Suez were consolidated with the producing and refining interests of that company on Bahrain Island in the Persian Gulf off the shore of Arabia. This led to the formation of the so-called Bahrain-Caltex group of companies, commonly called "Caltex," owned 50-50 by Standard of California and Texaco.

Concurrently, in 1936, Texaco purchased from Standard of California a 50-per-cent interest in California Arabian Standard Oil Company, holder of a vast concession in Saudi Arabia, which was later to become Arabian American Oil Company (Aramco). Also acquired from Standard of California was a 50-per-cent interest in a company holding at the time sizable concessions in Sumatra and Java, and an interest in a concession in Netherlands New Guinea. At the same time, an option was granted to Standard to acquire a one-half interest in Texaco's European marketing properties, but this option was allowed to lapse in 1939, because of the threat of war in Europe.

Entry into these areas was to prove more than just another landmark in the history of The Texas Company or, for that matter, the oil industry as a whole. The event had wider significance. Texaco and California Standard, through their affiliates, were among the first American oil companies to engage in fully integrated operations on a large scale in the Eastern Hemisphere. Their operations were to play an important part in the World War II effort of the United States. Moreover, these areas were to become important in the formulation of the Federal Government's policies in the Eastern Hemisphere after the war.

ARAMCO, AN AFFILIATE, IS DEVELOPING THE VAST OIL DEPOSITS OF SAUDI ARABIA

CRUDE FROM BARCO CONCESSION, COLOMBIA, BEGAN COMING TO MARKET IN 1939

9. Texaco
in World War II

To the armed services, nearly 6,000 employes;
to Government agencies, 700 more,
including the man who built "Big Inch" and "Little Inch";
to the Government, 30 per cent of the output;
to the bottom of the sea, 202 men and nine tankers

In 1939, Hitler sent his military might upon its mad career of world conquest. In the following year, western Europe was overrun by the Nazi war machine, and Hitler's air force launched the savage attacks that were intended to soften up Britain for invasion. The outnumbered British squadrons fought back, and they won the Battle of Britain in the skies. They could not have won it without the airplane fuel that had come from the United States.

In 1940, Mr. Rieber resigned as Chairman of the Board, and this position was eliminated by changing the by-laws. Col. Klein was given the title of Executive Vice President, in addition to that of General Counsel.

The year 1940 also marked the inauguration of Texaco's sponsorship of radio broadcasts of Metropolitan Opera performances, which has continued since then. Appreciation of these programs came from a large segment of the public.

When Pearl Harbor took the United States into the conflict in December, 1941, The Texas Company went on a war footing with the rest of the country. It became an instrument of the Federal Government for the salvation of the free world. The needs of the military services and of the nation's industrial machine that stood back of those services had first call on the energies of The Texas Company. Petroleum was as important in this war as gunpowder was in the Civil War. Almost two-thirds of all tonnage shipped overseas consisted of oil products.

Five thousand eight hundred and fifty-five Texaco employes (140 of whom, excluding ships' personnel, lost their lives) were drawn off into the armed services. Many others would have gone had not their skills been of greater use on the industrial front. Three hundred and seventy-three employes, who remained civilians, were drafted away from the Company for the duration to help man Government agencies. Three hundred and sixty-four others were temporarily drafted. In this way, the Company lost the services of some of its most important men. Many employes remaining with the Company throughout the war, from Mr. Rodgers and Col. Klein down, had additional duties with war committees, councils, and agencies.

This transformation took place with fewer hitches than might have been expected, because the nation and its major industries had been preparing for the worst since the fall of France, in 1940. Although we were not ready for war at the time of Pearl Harbor, we were more nearly so than ever before in our peace-time history. The other important factor responsible for the excellence of the oil industry's performance was the work of Secretary of the Interior Harold L. Ickes as Petroleum Administrator for War. He recruited his organization from the ranks of practical oilmen (The Texas Company supplied 50, on permanent loan), and he listened to their advice. The result was an outstanding example of industry-Government coöperation.

Each company, or group of companies, did what it could do best in the production of petroleum products for the war effort. Patented processes were freely licensed in a general effort to do everything and anything to help win the war. Competition for civilian business remained, but under heavy restrictions, including price ceilings. In the Spring of 1942, automobile gasoline was rationed along the eastern seaboard because of a shortage of petroleum transportation facilities. Later, rationing extended to the remainder of the country to conserve rubber.

FROM NECHES BUTANE PRODUCTS COMPANY'S PLANT, BUTADIENE FOR SYNTHETIC RUBBER

IN TWO WORLD WARS, ALSO IN KOREA . . .   . . . WE HAVE HELPED FUEL ARMED FORCES

EMPLOYES AT BAYONNE TERMINAL TURN OUT FOR LIBERTY LOAN PARADE IN WORLD WAR I

Like every other oil company, Texaco made what the Government told it to make. These included a number of things it had never made before—things that were no part of the business of the Company in peacetime.

By the time the war broke out, the Company was a leading manufacturer of aviation gasoline in the United States, its production of such fuel being exceeded by only one other American company. It was also a leading refiner of aircraft engine oils and supplied more than half the lubricating oil used on scheduled commercial airline flights in the nation.

During the four war years of 1942, '43, '44, and '45, The Texas Company produced aviation gasoline, 88.2 per cent of which went to the Government. It produced ordinary gasoline, 12.1 per cent of which went to the Government. This figure does not include the gasoline used in privately owned cars transporting workers to and from war plants. The Texas Company produced lubricating oils, 42.9 per cent of which went to the Government. It produced fuel oils, of which 45.3 per cent went to the Government. It manufactured a number of special products, such as toluene, butadiene feed stock, isobutane, butylene, heavy hydroformate, crude recycle benzenes, and the like, 100 per cent of which went to the Government. The manufacture of other old-line products, such as kerosine, gas oils, asphalts, waxes, roofing, coke, and so on, for which there was no great war demand, was continued as conditions permitted. About 30 per cent of all The Texas Company made during those war years went for war purposes.

It is impossible to say that any one thing was The Texas Company's, or the petroleum industry's, greatest achievement during the war. There were a dozen things without which, had they not been done and done right, the war would have been prolonged. Take the production of 100-octane gasoline for war planes, which the industry boosted from 50,000 barrels to 550,000 barrels a day—a tremendous achievement. Alkylate is an ingredient indispensable to the manufacture of 100-octane gasoline. Texaco was one of several companies involved in developing processes for its manufacture, and had a plant in California that had been turning out alkylate and storing it. When Pearl Harbor brought an immediate demand for more 100-octane gasoline in a hurry, this stockpile was exceedingly welcome. In the skyrocketing demand for aviation gasoline that ensued, the complete coöperation of Texaco and many other companies in the effort to give Uncle Sam the "gas" was a major contribution to the war effort.

All Texaco ocean-going tankers were taken over for war uses and Texaco participated with seven other major oil companies in War Emergency Tankers, Inc., a non-profit organization formed at the request of the War Shipping Administration to assist in operating oil tankers owned by the Government. The peak number of vessels operated by War Emergency Tankers, Inc., at one time was 105, of which 17 were assigned to The Texas Company. Texaco's 10 Norwegian-flag tankers were requisitioned by the Royal Norwegian Government in the Spring of 1940, shortly after the invasion of Norway, along with other Norwegian-flag vessels. Arrangements were made with the governmental authorities of Norway for Texaco to continue to operate these vessels.

Texaco tankers performed heroic service in every part of the world. Two hundred and two Texaco seamen and nine ships were lost through enemy action.

The exploit of one Texaco tanker that refused to sink despite savage enemy attacks received much publicity at the time and highlighted the hazards of wartime tanker runs. The ship was the *Ohio*, which the Government—through the War Shipping Administration—had requisitioned in June, 1942, and subsequently transferred to the British under Lend-Lease. Flying the British flag, and manned by a British crew, the *Ohio* left Gibraltar in August of that year in convoy. She carried a cargo of strategic fuels to Malta when, in the words of Winston Churchill (in whose war memoirs the *Ohio* is mentioned by name), that cargo was "vital" to the defense of the desperately beleaguered island fortress.

The *Ohio* was one of a convoy of 14 merchant ships, heavily escorted. So violently was the convoy attacked that one aircraft carrier and two cruisers protecting it were sunk. Seven of the cargo ships were sunk. Three of the remaining seven were hit. The crippled *Ohio* limped into Malta making only a little better than two knots.

On its own initiative, and without financial assistance from the Government, the Company had begun, in 1940, to build for its American-flag fleet several new tankers, with speeds in excess of commercial requirements. The purpose of the increased speeds was to render the ships more suitable as naval auxiliaries in the event of a national emergency. One of these fast ships was the *Ohio*.

In the Spring of 1942, before our defense against submarines was sufficiently developed in the Atlantic, tankers were sunk within sight of the Florida coast. The railroads were overloaded. Plans already had been made for getting crude petroleum to the eastern refining centers. After consultation with leaders of the industry, beginning in the Spring of 1941, Petroleum Administrator Ickes had determined to build, at Government expense, a 24-inch crude line from East Texas to Pennsylvania, with extensions to the New York and Philadelphia refining areas. Before that great work could be got under way, Mr. Ickes and his advisers decided on a second line, of 20-inch pipe, to carry refined products, principally gasoline, from Texas to New York. This was the genesis of "Big Inch" and "Little Inch."

The man selected to manage the construction was Burt E. Hull, president of The Texas Pipe Line Company, a Texaco subsidiary. Rough-and-ready old Burt Hull, one of the remaining few Texas Company executives whose service went back to Cullinan's day, had joined the Company in 1906 as a $75-a-month engineer. His first work was helping to survey the famous line from Tulsa to the Gulf Coast, the construction of which marked one of the turning points in the history of The Texas Company. Hull's performance in the building of "Big Inch" and "Little Inch" justified the reputation he bore as one of

LAUNCHED IN 1940, THE TANKER *OHIO* WAS VIOLENTLY ATTACKED EN ROUTE TO MALTA IN 1942

the world's great pipe line men. The first oil through the length of "Big Inch," which was completed in 350 days, reached the Philadelphia area in August, 1943. The main line was 1,254 miles long. Two hundred and twenty-two miles of feeder and distribution lines brought the total length to 1,476 miles. The volume of oil required to fill the system was 3,836,000 barrels, and 300,000 barrels daily could be delivered at the eastern terminals.

"Little Inch" was started later and finished in less time, the first gasoline arriving through the line at Linden, New Jersey, in March, 1944. This line was 1,714 miles long, including 239 miles of feeder and distributor pipe. Two million eight hundred and seventy barrels were required to fill "Little Inch," and it could deliver 235,000 barrels a day. Thus, in little more than a year, "Big Inch" and "Little Inch," built for $142,000,000, were in full operation.

The Texas Company played a significant part in the synthetic rubber program. America had long known how to make rubber artificially, but the supply of natural rubber was so plentiful that very little had been done with this knowledge in a practical way. When the Japanese cut off the supply from the Far East, we had to make artificial rubber in hitherto-undreamed-of quantities or lose the war. One of the prerequisites was a gaseous substance called butadiene, which can be produced from butylene, which is, in turn, a derivative of petroleum. The oil companies were prepared to produce butylene because it is essential to the manufacture of 100-octane gasoline. The demand for 800,000 tons annually of synthetic rubber, as well as for oceans of aviation fuel, made butylene a doubly indispensable strategic material.

Five oil companies with refineries located near one another in Southeast Texas exchanged their scientific knowledge, and altered their plants to turn out butylene in quantity—for rubber as well as for aviation gasoline. They were the Atlantic Refining Company, the Gulf Oil Corporation, the Pure Oil Company, Socony-Vacuum Oil Company, Incorporated, and Texaco. The five companies went a step farther. They organized a non-profit corporation called Neches Butane Products Company, which operated a mammoth plant for the manufacture of butadiene from butylene. The plant was erected by the Government at Port Neches, Texas. Rubber company plants in the area processed the butadiene with other ingredients to make rubber.

The hastily constructed Neches Butane plant, designed for a capacity of 100,000 tons of butadiene a year, actually produced 170,000 tons a year. It employed 1,000 workers. The five participating oil companies made no profit on this product. They received no fee for operating the vast plant. The president of the Neches Butane Products Company was a former employe of Texaco's Refining Department, as were the treasurer and an assistant superintendent. On the board of directors were two Texaco men, and in the plant and the laboratories were a number of experts on permanent assignment from the Texaco refineries. In all the industrial history of the war, it would be difficult to find a finer example of voluntary coöperation.

The Texas Company produced during the war 19,000,-000 gallons of toluene, a constituent of TNT, the high explosive used largely in bombs and ammunition, and for demolition. Prior to World War II, toluene had been made almost exclusively from coke. Production by this method would not have kept abreast of military requirements. An additional source of supply was developed from petroleum. Texaco spent more than $6,500,000 to equip its Lockport, Illinois, refinery for the production of toluene by a process known as hydroforming.

Because World War II was a global war, The Texas Company saw more of it than most American oil companies, by reason of the global nature of Texaco's holdings and operations. Its Caltex interests on Bahrain Island and the Aramco producing operations in Saudi Arabia put Texaco in a favored geographical position to contribute to the campaigns in Asia, the Pacific islands, and Africa, as well as those in Europe.

Caltex' widespread facilities were available to the Allied forces and, in some instances, were completely turned over to military use. Aramco was of vital assistance to our armed forces in some very desperate situations. For a time, as Rommel marched east across North Africa, it seemed as if the fortunes of war would shut off Middle East oil from use by the United States and its Allies. But in spite of this, Aramco determined to boost its output in every possible way. The company's entire output of crude oil was shipped to Bahrain, where it was refined and supplied directly to the Allied naval forces and War Shipping Administration vessels, or transported by tanker to various Caltex marketing areas engaged in supplying products for military operations.

The whole Caltex marketing organization in India, Burma, Australia, New Zealand, and Pacific islands became a part of the defense against the Japanese onslaught, which fell chiefly upon the United States sea and land forces. Some members of Caltex staffs in China and the Philippines were captured and interned for the duration of the war. Caltex tankers were sunk, and one was captured by enemy forces. When Bahrain, cut off from food imports, was threatened with famine, Caltex tankers carried wheat to the island for the general population.

All the while, the cry was for more and more production. The quantity of crude oil produced in Saudi Arabia was increased from about 12,000 barrels per day in 1941 to better than 58,000 barrels per day in 1945, an increase of almost 400 per cent. During the war, the United States Government urged Aramco to erect a large refinery with financial assistance from the Government. Aramco, however, in the darkest days of the war, on its own and without Government financing, undertook the construction of a 50,000-barrels-per-day refinery. It was completed and started operations in 1945.

Although the war was over by that time, millions of dollars had meanwhile been put into additional investment on Bahrain Island, likewise at a time when the war seemed all but lost to the Allies. This was done to increase crude oil production and expand refining facilities there. The Bahrain refinery, which in 1941 ran about 30,000 barrels of crude a day, had stepped this up to almost 63,000 barrels by the end of the war.

10. Postwar Progress

*Chairman Rodgers and President Klein are optimistic
at the end of the war. In the next five years,
almost a billion dollars for plant and equipment*

The surrender of Germany in May, and of Japan in August, 1945, brought a new series of problems to industry and to Government: reconverting the nation's industrial plant from a wartime to a peacetime basis, bringing home millions of men in the armed services from every quarter of the globe, and re-introducing them into the pursuits of peace.

Considering the magnitude of it, this operation went smoothly and swiftly. There was an immense demand for civilian goods of every kind, including houses for people to live in. The automobile companies had scarcely made a car for civilian use since Pearl Harbor. Within a matter of weeks after V-J Day, the first trickle was coming from the assembly lines. Gasoline rationing was off, and the oil companies had to meet the demand for fuel for old cars and new as Mr. Average Citizen could roll up to a service station and say, "Fill 'er up," without producing his "A" coupons.

When television caught the public's fancy after the war, Texaco sponsored Milton Berle on the "Texaco Star Theater," a television show which, like the Ed Wynn radio program many years before, made broadcasting history.

In April, 1944, the position of Chairman of the Board of Directors was re-created and W. S. S. Rodgers was elected to this post. Col. Harry T. Klein became President.

These two men had worked in greater harmony than perhaps any two top-ranking Texaco executives ever worked. Rodgers, the engineer and operating man, was freed of day-to-day matters and could look to the broad future needs of the Company and develop policies concerning them. He handled general policy matters, Government relations, foreign operations, and certain domestic operating problems. Col. Klein handled primarily the administrative, legal, tax, and other service activities of the Company.

Pivotal changes, revolutionary changes, were taking place that promised to affect the world economy of oil. Rodgers, Klein, and their scientific coadjutors determined to keep The Texas Company in the van of these developments.

In the Autumn of 1945, there were two schools of thought among American industrialists as to the immediate postwar future—one optimistic, and one pessimistic. Rodgers and Klein took the optimistic view. They believed that the oil business, in keeping with America generally, was in for good times. They acted upon that assumption, and have had no cause to regret it.

During the war years, Texaco spent $314,639,000 for additions to properties, plant and equipment, of which approximately $159,000,000 was spent for solely wartime facilities.

Although construction costs were two and one-half times what they had been in 1939, The Texas Company sketched out a five-year program which contemplated the expenditure of $500,000,000 for plant and equipment between 1946 and the end of 1951. It was figured that these capital outlays were needed to maintain Texaco's relative position in the industry, and help the Company forge ahead. Actually, The Texas Company executives underestimated the potentialities of their organization to get and hold new business. By the end of five years, capital expenditures amounted to $874,154,691, more than half again as much as had been planned in 1946.

Appropriations for the Producing Department nearly equaled those for all other departments put together. Before 1935, when conservation became effective, conditions tended to favor the refiner-marketer over the producer. About 1934, Texaco's management had begun to prepare for the changed conditions that would result from the conservation movement.

The Company's profitable operations over the last decade or more have been due, in no small measure, to the fact that it has been able to produce, on a gross basis, about three-quarters of its own requirements of crude oil.

This is the fruition of a far-sighted policy toward production that was inaugurated nearly 20 years ago, when additional funds for producing, or for anything else, were not easy to come by.

The next largest appropriations for the five years ending in 1951 were for refining, an expensive operation where the margin of profit has become narrow. Refining is highly technical and requires vast expenditures for plant facilities. In refining, moreover, there is unceasing pressure to better the product. This results in a high obsolescence factor in costly refining equipment, due to rapidly changing technology. The refiner has also the constant problem of the disposal of by-products, principally large volumes of residual fuel oil, the price for which fluctuates widely with general economic conditions. Residual fuel oil, which, at the close of 1951, sold for $1.65 a barrel in Oklahoma, sold for as low as 65 cents in 1949. Sales of residual fuel oil may represent as much as 10 per cent of a refiner's gross income.

To meet the booming postwar demand for gasoline and lubricants, in volume and in quality, called for a general overhauling and reconditioning of the whole refinery structure of the Company. The Philadelphia-New Jersey area has become a great refining area, second only to the Gulf Coast refining region, where 30 per cent of the country's capacity is located. Proximity of crude supply as well as proximity to the large eastern market were vital considerations. These factors were responsible for the erection of Texaco's Eagle Point Works, a 60,000-barrels-a-day refinery near Camden, New Jersey, which was opened in 1949.

Refineries were modernized and their capacities increased—Port Arthur Works, to 200,000 barrels a day; Lockport Works, to 65,000; Casper Works, to 15,000. Some small refineries were closed. The cost of modernizing several small plants would have been greater than to modernize one large one and build pipe lines to feed it. The growing importance of by-products favors the large plant over the small one. To obtain these by-products in sufficient quantity to warrant the installation of equipment to process them calls for a large refinery capacity. The capacity of the Lawrenceville refinery was raised to 47,000 barrels a day. That of the West Tulsa Works was raised to 35,000 barrels. Plans are on the drawing boards for the expansion and modernization of the Amarillo and El Paso refineries.

The moving of crude oil from fields to refineries, and of finished products from refineries to the consumer, continues to be an important item in the operation of Texaco. The transportation of petroleum products by large, ocean-going tankers, as well as by barges on inland waterways, is an economical method of getting products to market. Very often, however, The Texas Company cannot get its products within many miles of its customers by the water routes. Of the three means of land transportation—rail, truck, and pipe line—the cheapest is pipe line. The use of pipe lines is limited somewhat by their inflexibility, however. They require a guaranteed and steady source of supply at one end, and an assured and steady outlet at the other to be a successful proposition.

Nevertheless, since the war, The Texas Company has made heavy investments in pipe lines. Most of the new lines are larger than those generally in use before the war. Part of one consists of 24-inch pipe, the same as the famous wartime "Big Inch." Running at capacity, a pipe line 20 inches in diameter, for instance, can move about four times as much oil as a 10-inch line and consequently it is more economical to operate than the smaller line.

Also for the sake of economy, Texaco has joined in several projects with other pipe line companies to build pipe lines. Such a line is the Basin Pipe Line System, 517 miles in length, from Jal, New Mexico, to Cushing, Oklahoma. It is 20, 22, and 24 inches in diameter. The other participating companies are Shell, Sinclair, and Cities Service Pipe Line Company (formerly Empire Pipeline Company). With Shell, Texaco constructed the 22-

BEACON, NEW YORK: MAJOR CENTER OF TEXACO RESEARCH

CONDUCTING LAB TESTS AT BAYONNE, ABOUT 30 YEARS AGO

PRODUCING DEPARTMENT RESEARCH, BELLAIRE (TEXAS) LABS

inch Ozark Pipe Line System, from Cushing to Wood River, Illinois. Moreover, Texaco constructed lines on its own, the longest one being the 218-mile, 22-inch line from Houma, Louisiana, to Port Arthur, Texas.

The foregoing were crude-oil lines. The Company also constructed or participated in the construction of several products lines. One such project connected the refining areas of Beaumont, Port Arthur, and Houston with Fort Worth, Dallas, Austin, and San Antonio. In this way, The Texas Company moves its refined products from the Gulf Coast to Central, North Central, and West Central Texas. Another project is a products line from Casper, Wyoming, to Denver, Colorado. In pursuit of the postwar policy of fewer and larger refineries, the refineries at Craig, Colorado, and Cody, Wyoming, were closed, and the plant at Casper was enlarged and brought up to date. Also, parts of the refineries at West Dallas and San Antonio, Texas, which had become stations on the products pipe line just mentioned, were shifted to operation as sales terminals.

On the water, there has been a great development in the use of barges since the war. A substantial volume of bulk oil products is moved by tugs and tank barges to Texaco terminals in and about the various East Coast, West Coast, and Gulf Coast harbors, as well as on the New York State Barge Canal. Also, since the war, operations on the greater Mississippi River system have increased by more than 100 per cent. High-speed, integrated barge tows, averaging about 40,000 barrels capacity, equal to about 200 average-size railroad tank cars, transport Texaco products from as far south as Port Arthur to points as far north as Knoxville, Pittsburgh, Chicago, and St. Paul.

On the ocean, the demand has been for larger and speedier tankers. In 1949, the Company took delivery of four large supertankers, each with a capacity of approximately 200,000 barrels and a speed of 16 knots. In addition, there are Texaco tankers designed to carry as many as 20 different grades of products. At the close of 1951, Texaco had in foreign and domestic service 33 ocean-going vessels of 5,000 gross tons or over—the same number as at the end of 1945. But the deadweight tonnage was 544,283, as against a total of 430,922 five years before.

Since the war, the Domestic Sales Department has increased sales to more than 6,500,000,000 gallons annually. Each year new sales records have been established, both as to volume and revenue. The Texaco Credit Card has been a major factor in increasing sales volume. First introduced nationally in 1935, Texaco Credit Cards are honored throughout the United States and Canada at all outlets selling Texaco products. At the close of 1951, more than 400,000 active credit card customers were purchasing nearly $100,000,000 of Texaco products a year.

Postwar construction of product pipe lines, establishment of pipe line and marine terminals, and consolidation of existing bulk plants have improved methods of transportation and distribution and reduced operating costs. During the five-year period 1946-51, substantial improvement has also been made in Texaco retail outlets through the addition of 1,817 modern service stations and rehabilitation of existing stations. As a result, Texaco service stations throughout the country are in the main modern and well equipped to render the services present-day motorists need.

History is change, and this is true of the petroleum industry as it is of everything else. When The Texas Company was born, in 1902, the chief product of crude petroleum was kerosine. The use of heavy fuel oils was just beginning. Then, with the development of the automobile, gasoline, largely a waste product in earlier times, came forward to dominate the market. In 1952, it is still the most important factor in the business. In another 50 years, this may be true and it may not. Within the past 15 years, the significant development has been in petrochemicals—chemicals for which petroleum provides the major raw material.

The Texas Company continues to be an increasingly important participant in the petrochemical industry through Jefferson Chemical Company, Inc. This company is active in the production of synthetic chemicals from refinery gases. Texaco and the American Cyanamid Company each owns a 50-per-cent interest in Jefferson Chemical.

The Jefferson Chemical plant at Port Neches, Texas, went into operation early in 1948. Gases, piped from the Texaco refinery at Port Arthur, form the basic raw material. Previously, these gases were used as fuel for boilers. Now they are turned into ethylene glycol, ethylene oxide, and many other chemicals which may be used in the manufacture of explosives, resins, and cellophane; in processing textiles and tobacco; and as an ingredient for brake fluids. Ethylene glycol is the chief component of a permanent-type antifreeze for motor cars, which The Texas Company has been marketing in recent years. Ethylene oxide is used in making synthetic rubber, household and commercial detergents, plastics, and many other products.

As far as The Texas Company is concerned, it buys only ethylene glycol for antifreeze from Jefferson Chemical. Jefferson markets its products itself, and has American Cyanamid's experience in that field to draw upon. The young company is growing. It applies much of its income to further research in the domain of petrochemicals, whose future seems almost boundless.

Reconversion is not a strong enough word to describe the processes that were necessary to start to put Europe and the devastated Pacific areas back on their feet economically. They are not entirely on their feet at this writing, because of opposition stemming from the Soviet drive for world dominance, which thrives on economic chaos and the resulting human helplessness and misery. American private industry has played an indispensable part in the reconstruction and the rehabilitation of the economic pattern of a broken-up world. This process called for oil—oil in even greater quantities than did the war which wrought the havoc. In the production of this oil, the major contribution of The Texas Company has been through its interests in Bahrain and Saudi Arabia.

It will be recalled that the Bahrain enterprise has been developed since 1936 by the Bahrain-Caltex group of companies, owned half-and-half by The Texas Company and Standard of California. That ownership still prevails. The great increase in the production of crude petroleum and its derivatives that Caltex

AT BAHRAIN, A CALTEX TANKER TAKES ON PRODUCTS FOR SHIPMENT TO THE U. S. NAVY

THIS SAUDI ARAB IS ONE OF ARAMCO'S REFINERY WORKERS

brought about for war purposes proved inadequate to the demands of peace. Crude production on Bahrain Island rose from 22,000 barrels per day in 1946 to 30,000 barrels per day in 1951. The Bahrain refinery took care of all this production, and much more that was brought in from Aramco wells in Saudi Arabia. Refinery runs increased from 93,000 barrels per day in '46 to more than 180,000 barrels per day in 1951.

The growth of Aramco since the war has been enormous. Production increased from 164,000 barrels per day in 1946 to nearly 762,000 barrels per day in 1951. Refinery runs increased from 80,000 barrels per day to 159,000 barrels per day during the same period. It became obvious that the heavy burden of investment needed to develop the Arabian concession would severely strain the two parent companies. Consequently, Texaco and California Standard, after extended negotiations, agreed to an arrangement whereby a 30-per-cent interest in Aramco was acquired by Jersey Standard and a 10-per-cent interest by Socony-Vacuum, both of which had been active in developing Middle East oil but still desired access to more. This not only divided the risks of the venture but provided additional market outlets for Arabian crude, to the great advantage of the Saudi Arabian government.

Following an agreement reached in December, 1946, Caltex purchased, on January 1, 1947, Texaco's European subsidiaries, principally marketing companies. It could then truly be said that Caltex had spread its operations throughout most of the Eastern Hemisphere outside of Soviet Russia and Communist-controlled areas. As during the war, Caltex has continued to be a heavy supplier of products to the United States Navy.

A pivotal development in the history of the oil industry in the United States, which was essential in meeting the critical oil needs for the recovery of Europe, had its effect on the postwar history of Aramco and Caltex. Until 1947, United States production (except for the period 1920-22) had been sufficient to supply the American market and leave a surplus for export. Principally, this went to western Europe. In 1947, United States consumption exceeded production. The nation had to import to meet domestic needs. Fortunately, reserves were near by, in the Caribbean area. Western Europe, however, drew on the Middle East for oil that had previously come from America.

This situation led to the construction by the Trans-Arabian Pipe Line Company (owned by Texaco, California Standard, Jersey Standard, and Socony-Vacuum) of a large pipe line from Saudi Arabia to the eastern Mediterranean—the most difficult engineering and construction feat of its kind ever accomplished. "Tapline," as the company is called for short, brought the markets of western Europe 3,500 miles nearer to the oil fields. It transports crude oil for ultimate delivery to Caltex refineries in Europe and to other customers.

In December, 1950, the Trans-Arabian pipe line was completed and Arabian crude was loaded aboard the first tanker at the ancient Biblical port of Sidon, in Lebanon, the Mediterranean terminus. With its gathering system, which is owned by Aramco, the line is about 1,100 miles long. The capacity is in excess of 300,000 barrels a day. The line has in effect released 65 tankers for service on other routes. Hitherto, they had had to make the long haul through the Persian Gulf, the Arabian Sea, and the Red Sea into the Mediterranean via the Suez Canal.

Construction started at the same time at both ends. Seven hundred and fifty miles of the route lay through absolute desert, without roads and without water. Roads had to be built to transport the 93-foot lengths of 30- and 31-inch pipe in 50-ton loads. Special trucks to carry these loads were constructed on order. The tires on them were so large that a winch was required to change one. Wells were drilled along the route to supply water to the field force which, at its peak, comprised 1,557 Americans and 14,559 nationals of the four countries the line traverses— Saudi Arabia, Syria, Jordan, and Lebanon.

At the Persian Gulf end, a port and work shops were built on the desert coast, 125 miles from the nearest habitation, and 40 miles from the nearest drinkable water. It appears on the map as Ras el Misha'ab. The Gulf is shallow, and heavily laden ships could come no nearer than two and one-half miles off the shore. Lighter material was taken ashore in barges, but the sections of pipe went on "skyhooks," or overhead cables, an adaptation of a logging practice in Washington and Oregon for getting great timbers off mountain slopes. Two sizes of pipe—30 and 31 inches in diameter—were used to save shipping space, the smaller sections being "nested" within the larger. In the smaller sections themselves, cement and other materials were stowed.

The road that parallels the line is kept up for the line's maintenance. It connects the desert pumping stations. Each of these stations is a man-made oasis, with water wells, storage tanks for water, and facilities for watering the camels, sheep, and livestock that the Bedouins drive along the roads during their seasonal migrations. It has been estimated that during the Summer of 1950 Tapline supplied free water to 150,000 camels, and perhaps double that number of sheep and goats. The road also has become a highway for the movement of Mediterranean fruits, vegetables, and other commodities to Persian Gulf markets.

THE TRANS-ARABIAN LINE IS PATROLLED DAILY BY AUTO AND PLANE

11. It's the Future That Counts

The men who manage The Texas Company
are too busy these days to dwell on the past

So much, briefly, for the salient features of the prosperity and progress of The Texas Company since the close of global hostilities in 1945. The prosperity can be measured in dollars. Assets at the end of '45 stood at $833,853,650. In 1947, the Company crossed the billion-dollar mark. At the close of 1951, its total assets were $1,549,420,985. Earnings in 1945 were $51,856,928. In 1951, they were $178,774,677. Dividends have increased from $1.25 a share in 1945 to $3.05 a share in 1951. (These dividend figures are adjusted to take account of a two-for-one stock split in 1951.) At the close of 1951, the number of stockholders was 113,642, an increase of more than 20,000 since 1945. The Korean conflict, beginning in June, 1950, moved the United States and the rest of the free world back toward a war economy.

Since The Texas Company began entering foreign fields for other than sales purposes, the value of its holdings abroad has risen to more than $260,000,000. However, if these holdings outside the continental United States were swept away, the Company would lose only about 18 per cent of its total assets.

The progress of The Texas Company has been more important than its prosperity. Postwar years, to the close of 1951 anyhow, have been flush years. Nearly all business has been prosperous, and this has been particularly true of the oil business. It has been relatively easy for a currently well-run organization to make money. True progress is something else. It embraces a corporation's obligation, not to its owners alone—that is, its stockholders—but to society as well. The officers of The Texas Company have paid as much attention to that feature of their responsibilities as to the business of making money. The Texas Company has kept in the front of the profound technological changes that are transforming the industry. Its officers have kept in mind the uncertain future of the world, as concerns the issue of peace or war.

The general picture of success which runs throughout The Texas Company's history reflects its vigorous research activities. The Company's policy has always been to carry on its research so as to maintain its leadership in new methods of finding and producing petroleum, developing the best products, and manufacturing these products most effectively.

A program of employe benefit plan amendment and expansion, begun in 1937, is still in progress. Employes receive paid vacations, accident and sick benefits, and permanent total disability benefits, all at the expense of the Company. The costs of hospital and surgical benefits, and of group life insurance and pensions, are met jointly by the Company and the employe, with the Company assuming the major portion of the cost. Pensions are based on length of service and the pay of the pensioner while in active service. The contributions to the pension plan to cover the years of service prior to its installation on July 1, 1937, were made entirely by the Company.

To meet increased living costs, the Company began making additional payments to pensioners in 1948, so that an employe who retired after 20 years of service, but before 25 years of service, would be assured of a minimum monthly income of $75, and one who retired after 25 years of service would receive a minimum of $100 a month.

In 1952, the Company inaugurated a savings plan for employes. Under this plan, any eligible employe may authorize deductions from his pay of from two to five per cent each month. For every dollar the employe puts up, the Company contributes 50 cents. The entire amount is placed in the hands of a trustee, who invests it, at the employe's option, in United States Savings Bonds, Texaco stock, or the stock of certain selected investment trusts.

Early in 1952, there was another major shift in the top management of The Texas Company. Col. Klein moved into the re-created post of Chairman of the Executive Committee, and J. S. Leach, who started with Texaco in Dallas in 1916, was elected President. Mr. Leach, one of the many Texaco executives whose entire business careers have been spent with The Texas Company, is a native Texan. He rose through the Sales Department ranks until, in 1929, he became Manager of its Southern Territory. In 1938, he was elected Vice President of the Company with headquarters in Houston. He became Executive Vice President in 1950 and moved his headquarters to New York.

Today, The Texas Company faces the uncertain future with confidence. In a nutshell, these are the reasons: its high production rate, its efficient distributing system, its organization.

Possibly, as concerns the Company's future, the most important single factor—next to Texaco personnel—is the reserves of oil and gas in the ground that the management has accumulated during the past 20 years. During these years, the Company has made a great effort, and a successful one, to increase its domestic reserves as well as its foreign reserves. With the sale of a portion of its interest in Aramco, and with its investment in Aramco and in the Bahrain-Caltex group of companies beginning to pay off, The Texas Company had more money to build up domestic reserves in the United States, Canada, and South America. At the close of 1951, the Company's domestic reserves of crude oil and natural gas liquids were estimated at 1,852,000,000 barrels. Crude reserves of subsidiaries in foreign countries and the Company's net equity in domestic and foreign reserves of affiliated companies were estimated at 4,741,000,000 barrels. The combined total reserves of the Company aggregated 6,593,000,000 barrels. At a dollar a barrel, these reserves are worth more than four times the total assets of The Texas Company. That fact of itself would seem to justify the assurance with which the Company starts its second half-century.

In ordinary times, when a successful man, or a successful company, gets to be 50 years old, the conventional thing is for the individual, or the company, to look back with a certain measure of self-gratification. This short account of the first 50 years of The Texas Company is, in a way, a part of the looking-back process. It has been written, however, not by anyone connected with The Texas Company, but by an outsider. The people responsible for the recent years of the Company's success have been so busy looking forward and not backward that to get hold of them long enough to ask them questions that needed to be asked has not been easy.

Not that the men of Texaco's management do not take pride in their Company's history. They take an immense amount of pride in it, and that goes right down the line to the Texaco people in the field. It is a justifiable pride. Here they are, working for one of the world's great oil companies, which started in business on a shoestring 50 years ago, when the chances of success were about one in a thousand. But, as these are not ordinary times, there is little disposition among the top management of Texaco to dwell upon the past; and this because the present and the future are more important to them.

It seems to me that that is one more reason, and as good a reason as any, for believing that The Texas Company, like the United States of America, is going to have a future, a considerable one.

THE END

FOR THE FUTURE, INCREASING RESERVES OF OIL IN THE GROUND

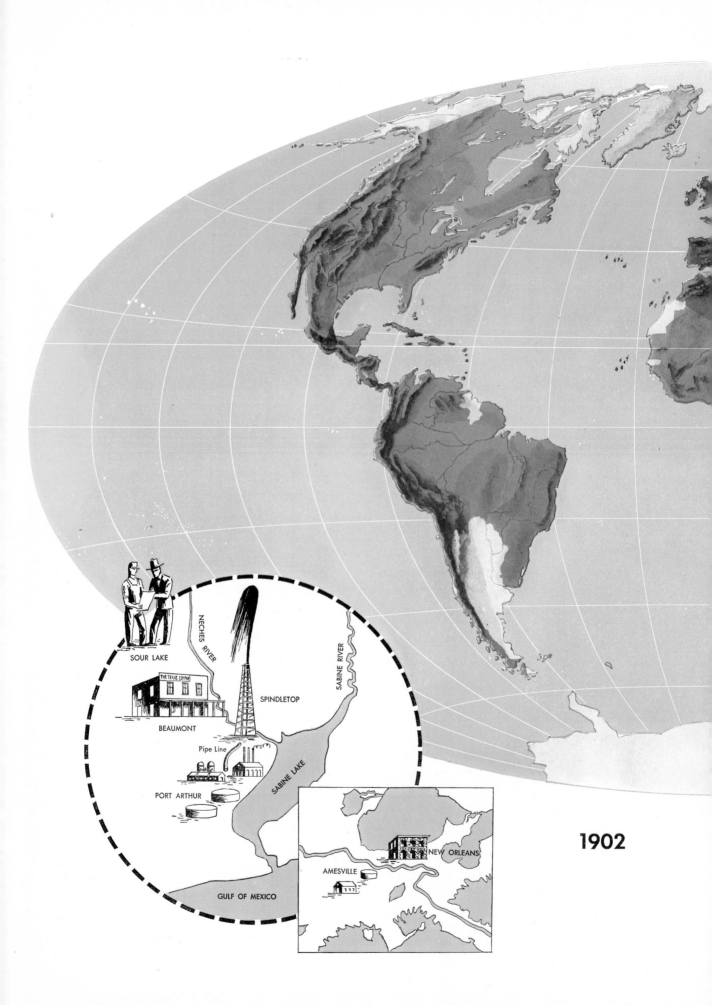

SOUR LAKE

NECHES RIVER

SABINE RIVER

THE TEXAS COMPANY

SPINDLETOP

BEAUMONT

Pipe Line

SABINE LAKE

PORT ARTHUR

NEW ORLEANS

AMESVILLE

GULF OF MEXICO

1902

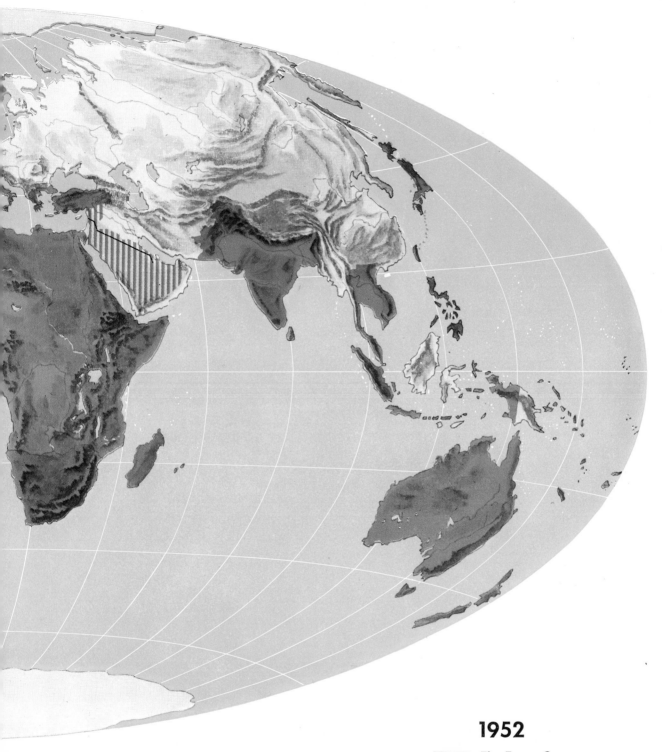

In the beginning, with the exception of a one-room office in New York City, The Texas Company operated solely in those areas of the South and Southwest shown on the small maps at the left. But since 1902, Texaco's fields of operations have continued to widen. Its boundaries broadened on the North American continent, stretched across the Western Hemisphere, and eventually spanned the oceans into the other half of the globe. Today, through subsidiaries and affiliates, The Texas Company operates internationally, as shown above.

1952

 The Texas Company or Subsidiaries

Affiliated Companies

 Caltex

 Other

 Tapline (including Aramco gathering system)

The Texas Company and Principal Subsidiary Companies

	Name of Company	Principal Business	Principal Areas of Operation and Percentage of Ownership
UNITED STATES	The Texas Company	Exploration, Producing, Transportation, Refining, and Marketing	United States
	The Texas Pipe Line Company	Pipe Line Transportation	Illinois, Indiana, Louisiana, Montana, New Mexico, Oklahoma, and Texas . 100
	Texaco Development Corporation	Patent Licensing	World-wide 100
	Valley Pipe Line Company	Pipe Line Transportation	California 100
CANADA	McColl-Frontenac Oil Company Limited	Exploration, Producing, Transportation, Refining, and Marketing	Canada; also Trinidad . 56.52
	Texaco Exploration Company	Exploration, Producing, and Pipe Line Transportation	Canada 100
CENTRAL AND SOUTH AMERICA AND WEST AFRICA	Texaco, Sociedad Anonima	Marketing	Mexico 100
	Texas Petroleum Company	Exploration, Producing, Transportation, and Refining	Colombia, Venezuela . 100
		Marketing	Colombia and Central America; West Africa . 100
	The Texas Company (Caribbean) Ltd.	Marketing	Haiti, Jamaica, and Dominican Republic . 100
	The Texas Company (Overseas) Ltd.	Marketing	Guatemala 100
	The Texas Company (Panama) Incorporated	Marketing	Republic of Panama
		Marine Transportation	World-wide 100
	The Texas Company (Puerto Rico) Inc.	Marketing	Puerto Rico and West Indies . . . 100
	The Texas Company (South America) Ltd.	Marketing	Brazil 100
	The Texas Company (Uruguay) Sociedad Anonima	Marketing	Uruguay 100
	The Texas Company (West Indies) Limited	Marketing	Cuba 100

Principal Affiliated Companies

	Name of Company	Principal Business	Principal Areas of Operation and Percentage of Ownership
UNITED STATES	Carthage Hydrocol, Inc.	Synthetic Gasoline	Texas 48.82
	Coltexo Corporation	Natural Gasoline and Carbon Black	Louisiana and Texas . 49
	Jefferson Chemical Company, Inc.	Chemicals	Texas 50
	Kaw Pipe Line Company	Pipe Line Transportation	Kansas 33.33
	Seaboard Oil Company of Delaware	Producing	California, Texas, Arkansas, and Wyoming; also Canada 32.31
	Texas-New Mexico Pipe Line Company	Pipe Line Transportation	New Mexico and Texas 45
	The Texas-Empire Pipe Line Company	Pipe Line Transportation	Illinois, Indiana, Kansas, and Oklahoma . . . 50
	Wyco Pipe Line Company	Pipe Line Transportation	Colorado and Wyoming 40
SOUTH AMERICA	Colsag Corporation (Barco Concession)	Exploration, Producing, Refining, and Transportation, through Subsidiaries	Colombia 50
	Sociedad Anonima Petrolera Las Mercedes	Exploration, Producing, and Pipe Line Transportation	Venezuela 50
	Venezuela Gulf Refining Company	Refining	Venezuela 33.32
EASTERN HEMISPHERE	Arabian American Oil Company	Exploration, Producing, and Refining	Saudi Arabia 30
	African Petroleum Terminals, Ltd.	Oil Storage	West Africa 50
	American Overseas Petroleum Limited	Exploration	Eastern Hemisphere . 50
	California Texas Corporation and Affiliates	Refining and Marketing	Eastern Hemisphere . 50
	N. V. Caltex Pacific Petroleum Maatschappij	Exploration and Producing	Indonesia 50
	Overseas Tankship Corporation and Affiliates	Marine Transportation	World-wide 50
	The Bahrain Petroleum Company Limited	Exploration, Producing, and Refining	Bahrain Island (Persian Gulf) . . . 50
	Trans-Arabian Pipe Line Company	Pipe Line Transportation	Middle East 30

April 7, 1952

Directors and Elected Officers
April 22, 1952

W. S. S. Rodgers*
Chairman of the Board of Directors

Harry T. Klein*
Chairman of the Executive Committee

J. S. Leach
President and Director

Augustus C. Long
Executive Vice President and Director

John Sayles Leach was born in Allen, Texas, September 30, 1891. He was graduated from Baylor University and came to Texaco in the Sales Department's Dallas office in 1916. By 1925, he had advanced to Superintendent of Sales, Dallas District, and four years later became Manager, Southern Territory. He was elected Vice President in 1938, with headquarters in Houston. In 1949, he was elected a Director; in 1950, Executive Vice President; on April 22, 1952, President. He is a director of Texaco Development Corporation, McColl-Frontenac Oil Company Limited, and Seaboard Oil Company of Delaware.

Augustus C. Long, a graduate of the United States Naval Academy, was born August 23, 1904, in Starke, Florida. He joined The Texas Company's Domestic Sales Department in 1930, after several years of naval service. From positions in domestic sales and foreign operations, he became Assistant to the Chairman of the Board, then (in 1949) Vice President in charge of Foreign Operations—Eastern Hemisphere. He was elected a Director in 1950 and Executive Vice President in 1951. Mr. Long is also a director of Arabian American Oil Company, Trans-Arabian Pipe Line Company, and Texaco Development Corporation.

*Biographies appear on Pages 60–61.

Continued . . .

G. N. Aldredge

Chairman, Executive Committee,
First National Bank in Dallas

Mr. Aldredge, who was born in Dallas and was graduated from Southwestern University, entered the banking business in Dallas in 1906.

W. J. Cummings

Chairman of the Board,
Continental Illinois Bank, Chicago

One of the nation's foremost bankers, Mr. Cummings began his career in banking in 1898 in one of the predecessors of the Continental Illinois Bank.

William S. Gray

Chairman of the Board,
The Hanover Bank, New York

A native New Yorker, Mr. Gray is an alumnus of Princeton University (Class of 1919). He has been an officer of The Hanover Bank since 1925.

R. F. Baker

Director and Vice President
in charge of Domestic Producing

A graduate of Sheffield Scientific School, Yale University, Mr. Baker came to work for Texaco as a Geologist at Tulsa, Oklahoma, in June, 1916.

Henry U. Harris

Member,
Harris, Upham & Co., New York

Mr. Harris, a stock broker, was born in Chicago. Following his graduation from Harvard University in 1923, he entered the stock brokerage business.

J. H. Lapham

Industrialist

Born in New York City, Mr. Lapham now resides in San Antonio, Texas. He has been a Director longer than any other Texaco Board member.

Charles L. McCune

President,
The Union National Bank of Pittsburgh

Mr. McCune, whose father and both grandfathers were active in oil and banking, left Princeton to go to work as a clerk in a bank in Pittsburgh.

M. Halpern

Director and Vice President
in charge of Refining

Mr. Halpern received a degree in civil engineering at New York University. He entered the employ of The Texas Company at Bayonne in 1916.

W. H. Mitchell

Member,
Mitchell, Hutchins & Co., Chicago

A stock broker and a native Chicagoan, Mr. Mitchell attended Harvard. Before entering the brokerage business in 1919, he had worked in a bank.

L. J. Norris

Chairman of the Board,
State Bank of St. Charles, Illinois

Mr. Norris was born in Elgin, Illinois. A graduate of the Chicago Academy of Fine Arts, he first worked as an artist, has been a banker since 1931.

R. C. Shields

Director and Officer,
Fisher and Company, Detroit

Mr. Shields attended Wharton School, University of Pennsylvania. In 1927, he joined Fisher and Company (engaged in real estate, investments).

R. L. Saunders

Director and Vice President
in charge of Domestic Sales

Mr. Saunders' only employer has been Texaco, which he joined in 1909. He became Chief Accountant, Northern Territory Sales, at age 25.

Other Elected Officers

G. R. Bryant
Vice President,
Houston

Mr. Bryant, who majored in civil engineering and geology at the University of Missouri, came to Texaco in 1937 from Indian Refining Company.

O. J. Dorwin
Vice President and
General Counsel

Mr. Dorwin received his law degree from Harvard. He was with the Indian Refining Company until 1934, when he was transferred to Texaco.

A. N. Lilley
Vice President,
Foreign Operations—
Eastern Hemisphere

A Californian, Mr. Lilley joined Texaco in 1933. His experience includes assignments overseas and in this country.

L. H. Lindeman
Vice President,
Finance and Economics

Mr. Lindeman began his business career as a stenographer; later, he studied law. He started with The Texas Company's Credit Department in 1910.

A. M. Ottignon
Vice President,
Supply and Distribution

Mr. Ottignon started with The Texas Company in 1915, at the age of 15, as an Office Boy in the Terminal Division of the Refining Department.

James H. Pipkin
Vice President,
Industrial and Public Relations

A Texan, Mr. Pipkin attended Texas A. & M. College and University of Texas Law School. He was employed in the Legal Department in 1934.

Torrey H. Webb
Vice President,
Los Angeles

A graduate of the Columbia School of Mines, Mr. Webb came to Texaco as a Statistician in 1922, by way of a subsidiary operating in California.

J. T. Wood, Jr.
Vice President,
Foreign Operations—
Western Hemisphere

Mr. Wood joined Texaco as a District Geologist in 1929. He is a graduate of Stanford's Geology and Mining Department.

W. G. Elicker
Secretary

After his graduation from Pennsylvania State Teachers College, Mr. Elicker taught school for 10 years before he joined The Texas Company in 1918.

Robert Fisher
Treasurer

Mr. Fisher, who was born in New York City, started with the Company as Office Boy in 1910. He has always served in the Treasury Department.

E. C. Breeding
Comptroller

When Mr. Breeding came to work for Texaco in 1921 as an Accountant, his background included experience as an employe of the U. S. Government.

Some Significant Texaco Dates

1901

The Lucas gusher came in at Spindletop Jan. 10 and started an oil boom.

Texas Fuel Company was organized Mar. 28.

1902

On Jan. 2, the Texas Fuel Company went into business.

Producers Oil Company was organized Jan. 17.

In February, the Texas Fuel Company opened its first office on Laurel Street, Beaumont, Texas.

The Texas Company was incorporated under the laws of Texas on Apr. 7.

The Texas Company's first pipe line from Spindletop was completed to Garrison, Texas, May 16, and to Port Arthur in August.

On July 1, the first New York office of the new Company was established at 8 Bridge Street. On the same day The Texas Company's first sale of crude oil was made in Texas.

In August, The Texas Company bought its first item of marine equipment, a barge.

The first terminal was opened at Port Arthur on Sept. 29. The Amesville (Louisiana) Terminal was opened soon afterward.

The word "Texaco" was first used as a product name Dec. 21.

1903

Texaco's third well at Sour Lake came in as a gusher Jan. 8, and the Company built a pipe line from Sour Lake to Garrison to connect with the Spindletop-Port Arthur line.

The first sale of a product—asphalt—was made in February.

Operations began at Port Arthur Works Nov. 3.

1905

Texaco organized the Continental Petroleum Company for foreign trade Sept. 29, with a terminal at Antwerp, Belgium.

Purchasing and Sales Departments were created separately from a department that had combined the two functions.

The first distributing station was built at Laredo, Texas.

1906

On Apr. 6, operations began at Delaware River (Delaware) Terminal.

Port Neches Works was acquired Sept. 1. The Directors resolved to double Texaco's capitalization Sept. 25, thus providing funds to link Oklahoma and the Gulf by pipe line. Stockholders authorized a $6,000,000 stock issue Oct. 17.

1907

In September, Providence (Rhode Island) Terminal began operations.

1908

The Texas Company's main office was moved from Beaumont to Houston.

1909

The first appropriation for advertising was made.

Manufacturing of cans began at Port Arthur.

In October, operations began at Bayonne (New Jersey) Terminal.

1910

Norfolk (Virginia) Terminal began operations on May 23.

The Export Department was organized July 1.

The Terminal Division was created in August.

West Tulsa (Oklahoma) Works began operations Sept. 1.

The Marine Department was established in October, with headquarters in New York.

Charleston (South Carolina) Terminal went into operation Nov. 1.

1911

Mobile (Alabama) Terminal began operations on Jan. 30.

The Sales Department was organized into territories and districts July 1.

Operations began at Lockport (Illinois) Works on Dec. 31.

1912

On Feb. 23, Jacksonville (Florida) Terminal opened for operations.

1915

On May 1, the Company moved into the new office building it had constructed in Houston.

1916

Producing leases were taken in Montana and Wyoming, and wells brought in in Wyoming, beginning Texaco's westward expansion.

The asphalt plant at Delaware River Terminal began operations July 13.

1917

The asphalt plant at Providence Terminal began operating on Apr. 18.

On June 26, The Texas Pipe Line Company, a wholly owned subsidiary, was incorporated in Texas.

The Texas Company absorbed Producers Oil Company on Nov. 13.

1920

The first Holmes-Manley thermal cracking units went into operation at Port Arthur Works on Feb. 8.

The W. H. Abrams Well No. 1, one of the most prolific wells in petroleum history, was brought in July 20 at West Columbia, Texas.

1922

Texaco began advertising gasoline in national magazines.

1923

Casper (Wyoming) Works went into operation on Feb. 6.

1926

Texaco New and Better Gasoline was introduced in May.

The Texas Corporation, a holding company, was organized Aug. 26.

1927

Texaco's State Cowden-Anderson Well No. 11 was brought in Aug. 9 in Crane County, Texas, and was to be one of the highest single producers of its time, producing an annual average of more than 1,000,000 barrels for the next few years.

1928

Texaco began operating Oakland (California) and Seattle (Washington) Terminals as of Jan. 1.

California Petroleum Corporation was acquired on Mar. 2.

Texaco began extensive marketing of Texaco Aviation Gasoline.

Marketing of Texaco products was extended to Canada with the organization of The Texas Company of Canada, Limited.

The Texas-Empire Pipe Line Company (in which Texaco took a 50-per-cent interest) was incorporated in Delaware in November to operate a pipe line from Oklahoma to the East Chicago area.

Amarillo (Texas) Works was acquired Nov. 1.

On Nov. 12, a contract was entered into with Louisiana Land and Exploration Company under which Texaco agreed to develop land in southern Louisiana.

Operations began at Portland (Oregon) Terminal on Nov. 28.

Texaco took over operations at Houston (Texas) Works, now Galena Park Terminal, Nov. 28.

1929

El Paso (Texas) Works began operations July 30.

The Texas Company (Overseas) Ltd. was organized Dec. 24, to consolidate foreign sales.

1930

Removal of the Company's General Offices in New York City from the Whitehall Building to the Chrysler Building was completed Apr. 7.

Texaco-Ethyl Gasoline was placed on the market.

The East Texas field was discovered in October.

1931

Majority control of Indian Refining Company was acquired Jan. 14 in an exchange of stock, and with it a refinery at Lawrenceville, Illinois.

1932

Texaco Fire Chief Gasoline was announced and the first comedy program on a nationwide radio hookup, starring Ed Wynn as the "Fire Chief," introduced it on the air Apr. 15.

1933

On May 10, The Texas Company purchased an interest in Great Lakes Pipe Line Company (a gasoline pipe line from Oklahoma and Kansas to Illinois and neighboring states).

1934

Havoline Waxfree Motor Oil was introduced.

East Chicago Terminal began operations in May.

1935

Kaw Pipe Line Company (a crude oil pipe line in western Kansas, one-third Texaco owned) was organized in Delaware Sept. 13.

1936

The solvent dewaxing and furfural solvent refining plant at Port Arthur Works was enlarged to permit manufacture of New Texaco Motor Oil, which went on the market in May.

Part ownership in the Barco Concession in Colombia was acquired Apr. 24.

The Bahrain-Caltex group of companies (owned 50 per cent by Texaco) was formed; a 50-per-cent interest was purchased in California Arabian Standard Oil Company (later to become Arabian

American Oil Company—"Aramco"); a 50-percent interest was also purchased in a company which held concessions in Sumatra and Java. This latter company also held an interest in a company holding a concession in Netherlands New Guinea.

1937

An Accident and Sick Benefit Plan (*see Page 112*) went into effect Feb. 1.

Texas-New Mexico Pipe Line Company (45 per cent Texaco) was formed in Delaware Mar. 22 to acquire, by purchase from The Texas Pipe Line Company, a pipe line system from southeastern New Mexico and West Texas to the Houston area.

On Apr. 27, a Group Life Insurance and Pension Plan (*see Page 112*) was authorized to become effective July 1, replacing the former Death and Disability Plan in force since Jan. 1, 1919.

A Permanent Total Disability Plan (*see Page 112*) went into effect July 1.

1938

Crude oil in commercial quantities was discovered in the Dammam field in Saudi Arabia after several dry holes had been drilled.

On July 1, the discovery well of the Salem field in Illinois was brought in by Texaco.

Texaco Sky Chief Gasoline, a premium product, was introduced in October.

1939

A 263-mile pipe line (50 per cent Texaco), connecting the Barco Concession in Colombia with Covenas on the Caribbean, was completed.

A 43-mile pipe line was completed between the Dammam field in Saudi Arabia and Ras Tanura on the Persian Gulf.

Completion of a sulphuric acid alkylation plant at Port Arthur Works pointed the way to quantity production of 100-octane gasoline.

1940

Operation of a 3,000-barrels-per-day Aramco refinery began in November at Ras Tanura.

Texaco sponsored Metropolitan Opera broadcasts.

1941

Construction of a sulphuric acid alkylation plant at Los Angeles Works was completed.

At the request of the Government, Texaco agreed to build a toluene plant at Lockport Works.

To simplify its corporate structure and to promote greater efficiency and effect economies, on Nov. 1 The Texas Corporation merged into itself The Texas Company (Delaware) and caused The Texas Company (California) to transfer all assets

to it and then dissolve. The Texas Corporation then became The Texas Company, operating as such in all 48 states and the District of Columbia.

1942

With other companies, The Texas Company in March organized the Neches Butane Products Company to build and operate for the Government, on a non-profit basis, a plant to produce butadiene, principal ingredient of synthetic rubber. This plant, which was owned by the Defense Plant Corporation, was in complete operation on May 25, 1944.

With other major oil companies, Texaco organized War Emergency Pipelines, Inc., to build for the Defense Plant Corporation a 24-inch crude line and a 20-inch products line from East Texas to the Atlantic seaboard. They were completed in 1943 and 1944, respectively.

1943

In August, The Texas Company and seven other oil companies organized War Emergency Tankers, Inc., to operate ocean-going tankers without profit for the War Shipping Administration.

The Bahrain Petroleum Company Limited, at Government request, began to expand its refining facilities on Bahrain Island to supply the Government with 100-octane gasoline. The expansion was completed in 1945.

1944

Plans were initiated and a preliminary survey of topography and problems of water supply started for a pipe line from the Aramco oil fields across Saudi Arabia to the eastern Mediterranean.

A Hospital and Surgical Benefits Plan for employes (*see Page 112*) began Nov. 1.

On Nov. 22, Jefferson Chemical Company, Inc., was organized by The Texas Company and American Cyanamid Company for the utilization of refinery gases to make basic chemicals for the chemical and plastics industries, including ethylene glycol for automotive antifreeze purposes.

1945

The Trans-Arabian Pipe Line Company was incorporated in Delaware July 24.

A new Aramco refinery was completed at Ras Tanura in December.

1946

New and Improved Havoline Motor Oil was introduced.

Overseas Tankship Corporation was incorporated in the Republic of Panama to handle the marine transportation requirements of affiliates of The

Texas Company and Standard of California throughout the world.

The Velasquez field in Colombia was discovered.

1947

Texaco's European subsidiaries were sold to California Texas Oil Company, Limited (50 per cent owned by Texaco), on Jan. 1.

Construction of the Trans-Arabian pipe line was authorized in January.

The Texas Company became a billion-dollar corporation.

Texaco offered nearly 2,250,000 shares of new stock to stockholders on the basis of one share for five, raising nearly $100,000,000.

Construction began on Eagle Point Works at Westville, New Jersey.

Conditional subscription to a 30-per-cent interest in Aramco by Standard Oil Company (New Jersey) and a 10-per-cent interest by Socony-Vacuum Oil Company, Incorporated, was made. These subscriptions, which left Texaco and California Standard each with a 30-per-cent interest in Aramco, did not become effective until Dec. 2, 1948.

1948

The plant of Jefferson Chemical Company at Port Neches, Texas, completed late in 1947, began operations, and Texaco PT Anti-Freeze, made from ethylene glycol produced by Jefferson, went on the market.

A modern laboratory for geophysical and producing research was completed at Bellaire, Texas.

Purchase of additional stock in McColl-Frontenac Oil Company Limited gave Texaco a controlling interest in this Canadian company.

The field of television advertising was entered June 8, with Milton Berle on the "Texaco Star Theater," a weekly, one-hour video show.

Pipe line deliveries of crude from Mercedes field, Venezuela, to Pamatacual Terminal, began July 1.

1949

Texaco Texamatic Fluid for automatic transmissions was introduced.

Field exploration work interrupted by World War II was resumed on a large concession in Central Sumatra held by Texaco's affiliate, N. V. Caltex Pacific Petroleum Maatschappij.

N. V. Nederlandsche Nieuw Guinee Petroleum Maatschappij completed a 30-mile, eight-inch pipe line from one of the three oil fields in a 31,400-square-mile concession to the New Guinea coast.

Eagle Point Works began operations on Nov. 2. The Basin and Ozark Pipe Line Systems, about 45 per cent owned by The Texas Pipe Line Company, were put in operation. They transport crude oil from Jal, New Mexico, and points in Texas and Oklahoma, to Wood River and Patoka, Illinois, in a pipe line that is 20, 22, and 24 inches in diameter. Texaco initiated these projects, which were the first large-diameter pipe line systems to be undertaken by private capital in this country.

1950

McColl-Frontenac started construction of a new refinery at Edmonton, Alberta, Canada.

A 5,000-barrels-per-day refinery at Cartagena, Spain, owned in part by Caltex interests, began operations, and operations also began at a 20,000-barrels-per-day refinery at Pernis, Netherlands, and the rebuilt refinery at Bec d'Ambes, France.

The first postwar well to be a commercial producer in the Minas field, Sumatra, was completed.

Construction began on a refinery in Italy owned 50 per cent by Caltex.

Pumping of crude oil into the Trans-Arabian pipe line began in September, and 5,000,000 barrels filled the line in November, with first cargoes being taken off Dec. 2.

1951

The Texas Company became a billion-and-a-half-dollar corporation in March.

On May 1, an Industrial and Public Relations Department was established.

Texaco Exploration Company made important discoveries of oil fields near Edmonton, Alberta.

New oil fields were found in Colombia, Sumatra, and Saudi Arabia.

1952

A Hospital and Surgical Benefits Plan for employes' dependents (*see Page 112*) became effective Jan. 1.

Simultaneous dinners honoring retired employes and those with 25 years or more of Texaco service were held throughout the country on Apr. 7, The Texas Company's 50th Anniversary. The 5,909 guests were addressed over a nationwide telephone hookup by Chairman W. S. S. Rodgers and President Harry T. Klein, after an introduction by Executive Vice President J. S. Leach.

In May, the first cargo of crude oil was shipped from the Minas field of N. V. Caltex Pacific Petroleum Maatschappij in Sumatra.

A Savings Plan (*see Page 113*) began July 1.

Period Ended	Shares Outstanding, Equivalent to $25.00 Par (End of Period)	Number of Stockholders as of Dec. 31	Total Assets (End of Period)	Stockholders' Equity*		Gross Income
				Amount	Per Share**	
.... 1902	....	110	$	$	$....	$ ....
Apr. 30, 1903	120,000	134	3,458,902	3,138,036	13.08	....
Apr. 30, 1904	120,000	134	4,464,340	3,752,286	15.63	....
Apr. 30, 1905	168,000	213	6,006,220	5,097,733	15.17	....
Apr. 30, 1906	240,000	237	7,961,690	7,266,499	15.14	....
June 30, 1907	320,000	352	12,940,460	10,696,500	16.71	....
June 30, 1908	440,000	501	18,954,413	15,018,224	17.07	....
June 30, 1909	480,000	600	26,134,719	17,367,317	18.09	....
June 30, 1910	1,080,000	1,037	30,252,707	28,228,634	13.07	....
June 30, 1911	1,080,000	1,617	45,192,931	28,602,995	13.24	....
June 30, 1912	1,080,000	1,528	48,283,225	29,458,120	13.64	....
June 30, 1913	1,080,000	1,644	59,720,697	34,455,744	15.95	....
June 30, 1914	1,200,000	1,453	68,124,814	41,242,849	17.18	....
June 30, 1915	1,200,000	1,559	75,505,762	44,592,748	18.58	....
June 30, 1916	1,480,000	2,056	102,577,937	61,841,523	20.89	....
June 30, 1917	2,220,000	3,570	133,279,735	95,437,468	21.49	....
June 30, 1918	2,775,000	....	167,783,471	124,671,869	22.46	....
Dec. 31, 1918	2,775,000	4,597	175,436,861	127,701,892	23.01	....
Dec. 31, 1919	3,400,000	5,367	229,065,846	161,375,739	23.73	....
Dec. 31, 1920	5,200,000	11,821	301,252,760	236,533,499	22.74	....
Dec. 31, 1921	6,578,000	20,278	296,679,177	249,292,357	18.95	....
Dec. 31, 1922	6,578,000	25,094	277,983,107	258,926,397	19.68	170,748,957
Dec. 31, 1923	6,578,000	31,866	294,017,935	252,927,435	19.23	169,382,738
Dec. 31, 1924	6,578,000	32,935	288,261,126	259,651,709	19.74	192,138,362
Dec. 31, 1925	6,578,000	32,657	298,622,809	277,916,023	21.12	207,954,199
Dec. 31, 1926	6,584,000	31,003	328,340,443	293,128,708	22.26	236,017,634
Dec. 31, 1927	7,219,243	39,319	324,806,372	291,540,471	20.19	218,947,323
Dec. 31, 1928	8,443,354	50,520	461,818,364	369,347,614	21.87	272,784,310
Dec. 31, 1929	9,850,050	65,898	609,853,084	445,090,111	22.59	305,332,054
Dec. 31, 1930	9,851,151	74,970	581,897,346	429,503,129	21.80	294,760,806
Dec. 31, 1931	9,851,236	85,082	543,329,526	397,047,563	20.15	242,746,917
Dec. 31, 1932	9,486,417	89,716	513,751,979	374,630,191	19.75	235,688,231
Dec. 31, 1933	9,352,371	85,635	484,454,337	344,928,188	18.44	239,258,554
Dec. 31, 1934	9,349,773	84,986	474,842,418	336,977,277	18.02	280,756,013
Dec. 31, 1935	9,340,069	83,514	473,776,967	336,576,360	18.02	308,913,546
Dec. 31, 1936	9,336,739	78,154	540,148,688	374,365,350	20.05	347,445,452
Dec. 31, 1937	10,875,006	83,514	614,793,217	466,844,051	21.46	387,255,853
Dec. 31, 1938	10,876,882	86,380	605,360,644	470,043,599	21.61	359,398,452
Dec. 31, 1939	10,876,139	87,875	661,067,033	482,388,753	22.18	374,479,623
Dec. 31, 1940	10,875,994	88,452	675,196,768	482,348,012	22.17	358,778,721
Dec. 31, 1941	10,875,800	90,141	695,831,742	508,724,371	23.39	414,857,369
Dec. 31, 1942	10,875,626	89,962	719,533,342	533,109,911	24.51	418,843,290
Dec. 31, 1943	11,186,279	91,563	790,731,568	573,256,535	25.62	466,766,561
Dec. 31, 1944	11,244,660	92,402	833,532,968	602,473,081	26.79	554,114,162
Dec. 31, 1945	11,244,660	93,337	833,853,650	626,218,360	27.85	584,887,838
Dec. 31, 1946	11,244,660	92,864	916,432,473	665,598,842	29.60	595,479,374
Dec. 31, 1947	13,461,096	100,114	1,111,289,026	853,637,894	31.71	839,967,335
Dec. 31, 1948	13,797,624	103,442	1,277,093,761	978,999,405	35.48	1,121,920,774
Dec. 31, 1949	13,787,624	105,220	1,368,132,586	1,055,984,874	38.29	1,116,037,056
Dec. 31, 1950	13,774,991	106,940	1,448,712,495	1,128,335,685	40.96	1,309,283,450
Dec. 31, 1951	27,510,693	113,642	1,549,420,985	1,221,273,369	44.39	1,490,076,744

*Paid-in capital plus undistributed earnings employed in the business.

**Based upon the number of $25.00 par value shares (or the equivalent thereof for those periods in which par value was $100.00) outstanding at the end of each period, adjusted for two-for-one stock split in June, 1951.

| Net Income | | Percentage of Net Income to Total Assets | Cash Dividends Declared | | Percentage of Cash Dividends to Net Income | Net Income Reinvested in the Business | | Taxes*** | |
ount	Per Share**		Amount	Per Share**		Amount	Percentage	Amount	Per Share**
....	$....	....	$	$....	....	$	....	$	$....
303,036	1.26	8.76	165,000	1.25	54.45	138,036	45.55	....	....
794,250	3.31	17.79	180,000	.75	22.66	614,250	77.34	....	....
505,447	1.50	8.42	360,000	1.50	71.22	145,447	28.78	....	....
978,114	2.04	12.29	609,348	1.50	62.30	368,766	37.70	....	....
2,431,926	3.80	18.79	1,001,925	1.88	41.20	1,430,001	58.80	....	....
3,618,578	4.11	19.09	1,196,854	1.50	33.08	2,421,724	66.92	....	....
3,217,520	3.35	12.31	1,318,427	1.50	40.98	1,899,093	59.02	....	....
6,424,189	2.97	21.24	1,562,872	1.50	24.33	4,861,317	75.67	....	....
2,574,361	1.19	5.70	2,700,000	1.25	#	(125,639)	#	....	....
2,201,069	1.02	4.56	1,350,000	.63	61.33	851,069	38.67	....	....
6,617,729	3.06	11.08	1,620,000	.75	24.48	4,997,729	75.52	....	....
6,325,904	2.64	9.29	2,550,000	1.06	40.31	3,775,904	59.69	....	....
6,402,533	2.67	8.48	3,000,000	1.25	46.86	3,402,533	53.14	....	....
3,797,353	4.66	13.45	3,350,000	1.25	24.28	10,447,353	75.72	....	....
9,596,906	4.41	14.70	4,532,500	1.25	23.13	15,064,406	76.87	....	....
1,581,727	3.89	12.86	6,243,750	1.25	28.93	15,337,977	71.07	....	....
6,690,672	1.21	3.81	3,468,750	.63	51.84	3,221,922	48.16	....	....
9,182,780	2.82	8.37	7,718,750	1.25	40.24	11,464,030	59.76	....	....
8,581,668	3.71	12.81	12,475,000	1.44	32.33	26,106,668	67.67	....	....
388,600	.03	.13	18,057,000	1.50	#	(17,668,400)	#	....	....
6,588,972	2.02	9.56	19,734,000	1.50	74.22	6,854,972	25.78	....	....
8,197,582	.62	2.79	19,734,000	1.50	#	(11,536,418)	#	....	....
6,458,275	2.01	9.18	19,734,000	1.50	74.59	6,724,275	25.41	....	....
9,605,078	3.01	13.26	19,734,000	1.50	49.83	19,871,078	50.17	....	....
6,044,497	2.74	10.98	19,738,500	1.50	54.76	16,305,997	45.24	9,914,189	.75
0,029,406	1.39	6.17	21,180,916	1.50	#	(1,151,510)	#	7,168,247	.50
5,073,880	2.67	9.76	24,306,712	1.50	53.93	20,767,168	46.07	10,771,192	.64
8,318,072	2.45	7.92	28,494,459	1.50	58.97	19,823,613	41.03	11,194,797	.57
5,073,303	.77	2.59	29,553,211	1.50	#	(14,479,908)	#	7,671,592	.39
9,954,478)	(.51)	(1.83)	22,165,214	1.13	#	(32,119,692)	#	6,106,041	.31
2,161,841)	(.11)	(.42)	9,851,262	.50	#	(12,013,103)	#	6,206,152	.33
(491,004)	(.03)	(.10)	9,335,885	.50	#	(9,826,889)	#	6,756,584	.36
5,545,205	.30	1.17	9,348,821	.50	#	(3,803,616)	#	8,189,171	.44
7,065,037	.91	3.60	9,339,861	.50	54.73	7,725,176	45.27	8,771,653	.47
8,260,341	2.05	7.08	14,005,111	.75	36.60	24,255,230	63.40	12,862,967	.69
5,184,319	2.54	8.98	26,419,971	1.25	47.88	28,764,348	52.12	18,919,214	.87
4,737,697	1.14	4.09	21,750,321	1.00	87.92	2,987,376	12.08	16,194,654	.74
4,127,358	1.57	5.16	21,752,278	1.00	63.74	12,375,080	36.26	16,246,183	.75
3,911,886	1.56	5.02	21,751,988	1.00	64.14	12,159,898	35.86	20,423,857	.94
3,053,271	2.44	7.62	27,189,500	1.25	51.25	25,863,771	48.75	31,696,541	1.46
4,568,969	2.05	6.19	21,751,252	1.00	48.80	22,817,717	51.20	29,550,361	1.36
7,688,797	2.13	6.03	21,787,919	1.00	45.69	25,900,878	54.31	31,574,123	1.41
4,516,819	2.42	6.54	28,079,673	1.25	51.51	26,437,146	48.49	41,487,563	1.84
1,856,928	2.31	6.22	28,111,650	1.25	54.21	23,745,278	45.79	26,715,714	1.19
1,089,267	3.16	7.76	33,733,980	1.50	47.45	37,355,287	52.55	37,913,983	1.69
6,312,617	3.95	9.57	26,962,745	1.13	25.36	79,349,872	74.64	49,930,679	1.85
5,980,980	6.01	13.00	40,619,470	1.50	24.47	125,361,510	75.53	77,310,494	2.80
2,743,159	4.81	9.70	55,142,428	2.00	41.54	77,600,731	58.46	56,038,351	2.03
9,071,743	5.41	10.29	75,795,357	2.75	50.84	73,276,386	49.16	77,073,822	2.80
8,774,677	6.50	11.54	83,934,415	3.05	46.95	94,840,262	53.05	121,500,203	4.42

***Excludes state and Federal motor fuel and oil taxes.

#Dividends declared exceeded net income.

( )Indicates red figures.

Year	Refinery Runs to Stills in the United States (Barrels)	Gasoline Production in the United States (Barrels)
1902	....	....
1903	43,200	....
1904	318,364	3,759
1905	548,136	17,847
1906	925,191	20,471
1907	1,409,608	47,538
1908	4,085,821	157,518
1909	6,168,693	336,731
1910	8,564,644	830,433
1911	8,778,510	1,102,996
1912	9,880,171	1,154,692
1913	12,017,899	1,356,348
1914	12,949,797	2,182,548
1915	17,874,880	2,399,417
1916	19,681,154	3,174,200
1917	23,709,277	4,564,389
1918	23,318,045	4,673,826
1919	28,609,909	5,227,156
1920	31,418,286	6,595,398
1921	26,966,563	6,651,326
1922	27,706,562	7,351,917
1923	29,556,803	10,012,621
1924	35,919,830	14,355,194
1925	34,414,290	15,212,576
1926	36,558,944	16,293,214
1927	38,847,192	18,528,887
1928	55,898,040	25,204,020
1929	58,294,221	29,057,997
1930	58,459,866	28,414,494
1931	59,476,148	30,541,430
1932	60,210,743	30,046,913
1933	65,449,199	31,778,878
1934	71,150,367	34,058,084
1935	76,276,245	37,839,235
1936	88,139,748	42,844,989
1937	96,423,516	47,557,271
1938	94,864,697	47,436,027
1939	100,467,283	52,029,147
1940	101,661,217	51,935,527
1941	115,166,938	61,747,839
1942	101,198,601	48,750,688
1943	113,139,584	50,905,600
1944	132,711,934	64,428,831
1945	129,434,479	64,811,011
1946	132,710,392	68,413,768
1947	139,127,232	73,826,237
1948	145,978,509	76,829,199
1949	151,037,739	82,820,526
1950	136,922,017	71,992,443
1951	175,968,740	93,624,325

Gross Crude Oil and Condensate Production (Barrels)			Net Crude Oil and Condensate Production (Barrels)		
Domestic	Foreign	Total	Domestic	Foreign	Total
308,687	....	308,687	216,306	....	216,306
3,812,720	....	3,812,720	2,671,684	....	2,671,684
5,501,080	....	5,501,080	3,854,767	....	3,854,767
7,708,942	....	7,708,942	5,401,880	....	5,401,880
5,559,826	....	5,559,826	3,909,967	....	3,909,967
8,220,648	....	8,220,648	5,153,585	....	5,153,585
7,375,945	....	7,375,945	5,517,663	....	5,517,663
5,286,100	....	5,286,100	4,224,571	....	4,224,571
7,206,303	....	7,206,303	5,560,075	....	5,560,075
7,751,194	....	7,751,194	5,932,749	....	5,932,749
8,044,679	152	8,044,831	6,456,428	122	6,456,550
10,419,509	537,914	10,957,423	8,843,761	430,331	9,274,092
16,380,217	1,643,152	18,023,369	13,535,418	1,314,522	14,849,940
19,747,921	1,707,623	21,455,544	16,877,398	1,366,098	18,243,496
16,741,480	1,655,782	18,397,262	14,122,909	1,324,626	15,447,535
15,236,340	1,707,871	16,944,211	12,774,634	1,366,297	14,140,931
14,075,586	1,431,567	15,507,153	12,090,620	1,145,254	13,235,874
17,117,592	5,768,917	22,886,509	14,317,902	4,615,134	18,933,036
21,457,803	12,271,839	33,729,642	18,586,363	9,817,471	28,403,834
19,913,626	6,735,933	26,649,559	17,346,968	5,388,746	22,735,714
21,021,696	3,967,137	24,988,833	17,817,287	3,173,710	20,990,997
20,622,718	2,637,612	23,260,330	17,194,929	2,016,847	19,211,776
18,658,339	1,573,520	20,231,859	15,780,314	1,202,593	16,982,907
21,782,804	740,056	22,522,860	18,210,069	542,512	18,752,581
21,788,973	509,186	22,298,159	18,091,217	461,240	18,552,457
26,939,451	386,819	27,326,270	22,569,279	351,652	22,920,931
46,440,940	314,246	46,755,186	38,594,965	245,426	38,840,391
53,005,697	264,678	53,270,375	43,604,034	216,646	43,820,680
43,199,775	253,414	43,453,189	36,852,945	205,690	37,058,635
34,578,561	218,083	34,796,644	29,295,907	180,122	29,476,029
33,760,168	205,198	33,965,366	28,281,584	172,174	28,453,758
36,785,952	193,060	36,979,012	30,854,254	164,911	31,019,165
37,226,662	191,646	37,418,308	31,086,158	169,981	31,256,139
45,616,963	89,895	45,706,858	37,646,139	80,215	37,726,354
53,854,116	....	53,854,116	43,799,831	....	43,799,831
60,476,616	....	60,476,616	49,525,343	....	49,525,343
58,519,827	....	58,519,827	48,159,992	....	48,159,992
74,953,771	....	74,953,771	63,428,472	....	63,428,472
99,070,778	....	99,070,778	84,596,801	....	84,596,801
86,901,584	....	86,901,584	73,734,489	....	73,734,489
76,669,706	....	76,669,706	65,310,919	....	65,310,919
84,639,468	58,980	84,698,448	71,900,500	51,257	71,951,757
98,523,647	179,189	98,702,836	83,833,215	148,825	83,982,040
100,957,670	678,575	101,636,245	85,874,079	565,321	86,439,400
98,816,697	1,269,018	100,085,715	84,071,329	1,056,023	85,127,352
105,628,770	3,164,341	108,793,111	89,751,538	2,589,614	92,341,152
113,585,477	4,789,966	118,375,443	96,339,920	3,874,949	100,214,869
105,277,838	9,235,238	114,513,076	88,829,288	7,451,651	96,280,939
111,825,526	10,661,950	122,487,476	94,249,359	8,655,124	102,904,483
127,406,608	10,442,041	137,848,649	107,593,195	8,536,906	116,130,101

EMPLOYES and PAYROLLS—1923 to 1951, INCLUSIVE

THE TEXAS COMPANY AND SUBSIDIARY COMPANIES

Year	Average Number of Employes			Total Payrolls			Average Annual Rate of Pay Per Domestic Employe
	Domestic	Foreign	Total	Domestic	Foreign	Total	
1923	19,525	3,318	22,843	$ 34,038,846	$ 3,341,591	$ 37,380,437	$1,743
1924	16,902	3,009	19,911	30,931,733	2,727,412	33,659,145	1,830
1925	15,631	2,835	18,466	29,750,401	2,569,451	32,319,852	1,903
1926	16,212	2,800	19,012	31,355,416	2,554,564	33,909,980	1,934
1927	17,016	2,845	19,861	33,259,129	2,587,669	35,846,798	1,955
1928	21,127	3,186	24,313	42,921,974	2,963,452	45,885,426	2,032
1929	24,724	3,849	28,573	49,499,463	3,825,723	53,325,186	2,002
1930	21,833	5,248	27,081	45,377,957	5,322,051	50,700,008	2,078
1931	17,852	5,361	23,213	36,754,495	4,931,931	41,686,426	2,059
1932	17,515	5,308	22,823	31,976,718	5,282,842	37,259,560	1,826
1933	20,301	5,500	25,801	34,174,801	4,677,328	38,852,129	1,683
1934	23,328	5,584	28,912	38,628,068	5,793,400	44,421,468	1,656
1935	23,287	5,850	29,137	39,917,207	5,780,332	45,697,539	1,714
1936	24,444	5,051	29,495	43,619,195	4,894,978	48,514,173	1,784
1937	27,213	3,814	31,027	52,945,092	3,537,646	56,482,738	1,946
1938	26,496	4,221	30,717	53,519,971	3,730,578	57,250,549	2,020
1939	26,970	4,527	31,497	54,705,610	3,985,013	58,690,623	2,028
1940	27,298	1,964	29,262	56,130,520	1,767,531	57,898,051	2,056
1941	26,929	2,088	29,017	59,417,208	1,790,969	61,208,177	2,206
1942	25,553	2,021	27,574	64,203,398	1,917,754	66,121,152	2,513
1943	24,591	1,998	26,589	72,520,896	2,106,160	74,627,056	2,949
1944	25,817	2,238	28,055	82,353,207	2,705,145	85,058,352	3,190
1945	27,201	2,901	30,102	87,666,419	3,697,857	91,364,276	3,223
1946	30,430	3,787	34,217	99,808,902	5,913,162	105,722,064	3,280
1947	32,072	6,239	38,311	121,041,966	10,542,954	131,584,920	3,774
1948	32,900	7,305	40,205	136,244,807	18,250,893	154,495,700	4,141
1949	32,728	6,429	39,157	139,879,198	15,675,165	155,554,363	4,274
1950	32,245	6,001	38,246	134,883,842	15,115,775	149,999,617	4,461
1951	33,203	6,544	39,747	156,821,929	17,106,431	173,928,360	4,723

We've Kept Our Balance

Merely the figures of these two Texaco balance sheets (one of 1902 and the other at the close of 1951) make a breath-taking commentary on the growth and progress of The Texas Company in the first 50 years of its corporate existence. The Company's total assets have multiplied enormously. At the end of 1951, they were 855 times the $1,811,859.56—substantially all of which was assets—tabulated on the trial balance at December 31, 1902. Through December 31, 1951, 53 per cent of the total net income of The Texas Company had been declared as cash dividends and 47 per cent of the total net income reinvested in the business.

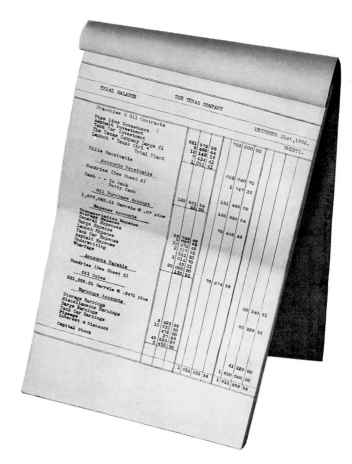

Employe Benefit Plans

In order to provide greater financial security for the men and women who work so loyally and effectively in the Company's behalf, and for their families, The Texas Company has established, over the years, a number of benefit plans. These plans are as follows:

Accident and Sick Benefit Plan

Provides full-pay benefits for a period and half-pay benefits for an additional period in the event employes are temporarily absent because of occupational or non-occupational illness or injury. Payment of benefits may be continued for as long as one year.

Group Life Insurance and Pension Plan

Provides life insurance coverage during employment, in an amount approximating 150 per cent of annual pay. Coverage after retirement approximates the employe's last annual pay.

Also provides for lifetime monthly annuity payments after retirement. These annuity payments are in addition to Social Security.

Hospital and Surgical Benefits Plans

For Employes and Dependents

Provide for reimbursement of specific hospital and surgical expenses incurred by employes or their dependents.

Permanent Total Disability Plan

For employes who become permanently and totally disabled, provides quarter-pay benefits for a period as long as 12 years and provides for Group Life Insurance coverage, during disability, in an amount approximating one year's pay.

The Vacation Plan

Provides for annual periods of time off, with pay, to afford employes an opportunity for rest and relaxation. All regular employes receive annual vacations with pay after one year of service.

In addition to the above Company-sponsored plans, employes are benefited by the following programs which are required by the Federal or state governments:

Old-Age and Survivors' Benefits (Social Security)

Unemployment Benefits

Workmen's Compensation covering occupational illness or injury

Of the foregoing plans and programs, employes contribute jointly with the Company to Social Security, unemployment insurance in a few states, and the Hospital and Surgical Benefits and Group Life Insurance and Pension Plans. The Company pays the total cost of the others.

Company Cost of Employe Benefit Plans, Social Security, Unemployment Benefits, and Workmen's Compensation —The Texas Company and Domestic Subsidiaries

1937	$ 6,993,697
1938	7,740,410
1939	7,837,831
1940	8,418,578
1941	8,045,130
1942	11,167,281
1943	11,417,034
1944	10,543,203
1945	10,831,320
1946	12,570,122
1947	17,157,257
1948	18,296,539
1949	21,245,254
1950	22,052,970
1951	27,254,811

Savings Plan

On July 1, 1952, the Employes Savings Plan, ratified at the Annual Meeting of Stockholders of The Texas Company on April 22, 1952, went into effect. Under the plan, the employe decides how much of his salary or wages he will save each month—the minimum is two per cent, the maximum, five per cent. The Company adds 50 cents to every dollar saved by the employe, and the employe determines how his savings and the Company's contributions are to be invested. He may put the entire amount in U. S. Savings Bonds, Texaco capital stock, in shares of certain investment companies, or he may divide it up among the three categories in proportions chosen by him. When an employe leaves the Company after 60 months of participation, or dies, or retires, he, or his beneficiary, will receive the cash or securities, with dividends or interest, accumulated in his account.

Directors and Elected Officers
THE TEXAS COMPANY (Delaware)
and Predecessor Companies
April 7, 1902, to April 22, 1952, Inclusive

DIRECTORS	R. E. Brooks	From	Apr. 7, 1902	To	May 31, 1904
			Nov. 26, 1907		Jan. 6, 1913
			Jan. 7, 1918		Nov. 18, 1920
	William T. Campbell		Apr. 7, 1902		Nov. 25, 1902
	Joseph S. Cullinan		Apr. 7, 1902		Nov. 25, 1913
	John W. Gates		Apr. 7, 1902		*Died Aug. 9, 1911*
	J. C. Hutchins		Apr. 7, 1902		Nov. 24, 1903
	Lewis H. Lapham		Apr. 7, 1902		Apr. 25, 1903
			Nov. 24, 1903		Mar. 16, 1926
	E. J. Marshall		Apr. 7, 1902		Nov. 25, 1902
	Roderick Oliver		Apr. 7, 1902		Nov. 17, 1903
	Arnold Schlaet		Apr. 7, 1902		Jan. 1, 1920
	Thomas J. Donoghue		Nov. 25, 1902		Apr. 24, 1934
	Fred W. Freeman		Nov. 25, 1902		June 13, 1905
	W. J. McKie		Apr. 25, 1903		Nov. 24, 1903
	Walter B. Sharp		Nov. 17, 1903		June 13, 1905
	James Hopkins		Nov. 24, 1903		May 31, 1904
	Clarence P. Dodge		May 31, 1904		*Died Jan. 13, 1926*
	W. T. Leman		May 31, 1904		Feb. 12, 1907
	James L. Autry		June 13, 1905		Nov. 25, 1913
	William A. Thompson, Jr.		June 13, 1905		May 29, 1906
			Nov. 25, 1913		*Died July 24, 1922*
	Ralph C. Holmes		May 29, 1906		Apr. 24, 1934
	Martin Moran		Feb. 12, 1907		Nov. 22, 1910
	W. S. Fanshawe		Nov. 26, 1907		Nov. 17, 1908
	John F. Harris		Nov. 17, 1908		Nov. 18, 1911
	Elgood C. Lufkin		Nov. 16, 1909		Apr. 28, 1931
	George L. Noble		Nov. 16, 1909		Apr. 20, 1927
	John J. Mitchell		Nov. 22, 1910		*Died Oct. 29, 1927*
	Alonzo B. Hepburn		Sept. 9, 1911		*Died Jan. 20, 1922*
	Charles G. Gates		Nov. 18, 1911		*Died Oct. 28, 1913*
	William C. Hogg		Jan. 6, 1913		Nov. 25, 1913
	Amos L. Beaty		Nov. 25, 1913		Dec. 21, 1927
	James N. Hill		Nov. 25, 1913		*Died July 3, 1932*

· 114 ·

DIRECTORS	John H. Lapham	From	Nov. 25, 1913	To	Jan. 7, 1918
			Mar. 21, 1922		Now serving
	Edwin B. Parker		June 3, 1920		Mar. 27, 1923
	Frank D. Stout		Mar. 31, 1921		*Died Oct. 11, 1927*
	Charles E. Herrmann		Dec. 12, 1922		*Died Dec. 20, 1924*
	Charles B. Ames		Mar. 27, 1923		Dec. 28, 1925
			Jan. 18, 1928		Nov. 22, 1932
			May 5, 1933		*Died July 21, 1935*
	Daniel J. Moran		Dec. 24, 1924		Nov. 27, 1928
	W. W. Bruce		Dec. 28, 1925		Mar. 20, 1928
	Henry G. Lapham		Mar. 16, 1926		Sept. 19, 1933
	Albert Rockwell		Mar. 16, 1926		Apr. 24, 1934
	Eugene M. Stevens		Jan. 18, 1928		Feb. 20, 1934
	George G. Allen		Mar. 20, 1928		Mar. 13, 1934
	Thomas A. O'Donnell		Mar. 20, 1928		May 22, 1928
	Jacques Vinmont		Mar. 20, 1928		Nov. 27, 1928
	William A. Fisher		May 22, 1928		Apr. 24, 1934
	Torkild Rieber		Nov. 27, 1928		Aug. 23, 1940
	W. S. S. Rodgers		Nov. 27, 1928		Now serving
	Rodolfo Ogarrio		Apr. 28, 1931		Dec. 27, 1950
	Harry T. Klein		Jan. 24, 1933		Apr. 24, 1934
			Apr. 23, 1935		Now serving
	Walter G. Dunnington		Sept. 19, 1933		Jan. 4, 1949
	William H. Mitchell		Sept. 19, 1933		Now serving
	Lester J. Norris		Sept. 19, 1933		Now serving
	Warren G. Horton		Mar. 20, 1934		Jan. 31, 1936
	P. H. O'Neil		Mar. 20, 1934		Apr. 23, 1935
	George N. Aldredge		Apr. 24, 1934		Now serving
	Walter J. Cummings		Apr. 24, 1934		Now serving
	William S. Gray		Apr. 24, 1934		Now serving
	Charles A. McCulloch		Apr. 24, 1934		*Died Jan. 24, 1946*
	R. C. Shields		Apr. 24, 1934		Now serving
	Henry U. Harris		Aug. 9, 1935		Now serving
	Barklie Henry		Jan. 31, 1936		Oct. 26, 1945
	Clarence E. Olmsted		Aug. 23, 1940		Aug. 4, 1950
	Charles L. McCune		Oct. 26, 1945		Now serving
	Michael Halpern		Feb. 8, 1946		Now serving
	Richard L. Saunders		Feb. 8, 1946		Now serving
	J. S. Leach		Apr. 26, 1949		Now serving
	R. F. Baker		Aug. 4, 1950		Now serving
	Augustus C. Long		Aug. 4, 1950		Now serving

CHAIRMEN*	Elgood C. Lufkin	From Mar. 23, 1920	To Mar. 9, 1926
	Amos L. Beaty	Mar. 16, 1926	Dec. 21, 1927
	Ralph C. Holmes	Apr. 25, 1933	May 5, 1933
	Charles B. Ames	May 5, 1933	*Died July 21, 1935*
	Torkild Rieber	Aug. 9, 1935	Aug. 12, 1940
	W. S. S. Rodgers	Apr. 25, 1944	Now serving
CHAIRMEN OF THE EXECUTIVE COMMITTEE	Arnold Schlaet	Nov. 17, 1914	Jan. 1, 1920
	John H. Lapham	Apr. 25, 1933	Apr. 24, 1934
	Harry T. Klein	Apr. 22, 1952	Now serving
PRESIDENTS	Joseph S. Cullinan	May 20, 1902	Nov. 25, 1913
	Elgood C. Lufkin	Nov. 25, 1913	Mar. 23, 1920
	Amos L. Beaty	Mar. 23, 1920	Mar. 16, 1926
	Ralph C. Holmes	Mar. 16, 1926	Apr. 25, 1933
	W. S. S. Rodgers	Apr. 25, 1933	Apr. 25, 1944
	Harry T. Klein	Apr. 25, 1944	Apr. 22, 1952
	J. S. Leach	Apr. 22, 1952	Now serving
VICE PRESIDENTS	Roderick Oliver	May 20, 1902	Nov. 24, 1903
	Arnold Schlaet**	May 20, 1902	Nov. 17, 1914
	R. E. Brooks	Nov. 24, 1903	May 31, 1904
	Elgood C. Lufkin	Nov. 16, 1909	Nov. 25, 1913
	Thomas J. Donoghue	Nov. 22, 1910	June 30, 1939
	John F. Harris	Nov. 22, 1910	Nov. 18, 1911
	George L. Noble	July 20, 1912	June 30, 1939
	Ralph C. Holmes	Jan. 6, 1913	Mar. 16, 1926
	William A. Thompson, Jr.	Jan. 6, 1913	*Died July 24, 1922*
	John R. Miglietta	Nov. 17, 1914	Nov. 18, 1920
	Clement N. Scott	Mar. 23, 1920	July 28, 1922
	Charles E. Herrmann	Dec. 12, 1922	*Died Dec. 20, 1924*
	Daniel J. Moran	Mar. 18, 1924	Nov. 27, 1928
	W. W. Bruce	Apr. 7, 1925	Mar. 26, 1929
	Charles B. Ames	Jan. 18, 1928	Nov. 22, 1932
	Torkild Rieber	Mar. 20, 1928	Aug. 9, 1935
	W. S. S. Rodgers	Oct. 1, 1928	Apr. 25, 1933
	Frederick T. Manley	Nov. 27, 1928	Oct. 27, 1939
	Rodolfo Ogarrio	Dec. 18, 1928	Dec. 27, 1950
	Henry W. Dodge	May 5, 1933	Sept. 1, 1945
	Harry T. Klein***	May 5, 1933	Apr. 25, 1944
	J. S. Leach****	Aug. 1, 1938	Apr. 22, 1952
	Clarence E. Olmsted	Aug. 1, 1938	Aug. 4, 1950

*The position of Chairman of the Board of Directors was not created until 1920. Subsequently, there were several periods during which the chairmanship did not exist.

**Was elected as First Vice President.
***Elected Executive Vice President Sept. 27, 1940.
****Elected Executive Vice President Aug. 4, 1956.

		From	To
VICE PRESIDENTS	Michael Halpern	Sept. 27, 1940	Now serving
	James Tanham	Sept. 26, 1941	Aug. 31, 1950
	Torrey H. Webb	Sept. 26, 1941	Now serving
	Richard L. Saunders	Apr. 25, 1944	Now serving
	Burton E. Hull	Mar. 7, 1947	May 31, 1951
	R. F. Baker	June 24, 1949	Now serving
	L. H. Lindeman	June 24, 1949	Now serving
	Augustus C. Long*	June 24, 1949	Now serving
	George R. Bryant	Aug. 4, 1950	Now serving
	James T. Wood, Jr.	Aug. 4, 1950	Now serving
	Oscar John Dorwin	Dec. 7, 1951	Now serving
	A. Neil Lilley	Dec. 7, 1951	Now serving
	A. M. Ottignon	Dec. 7, 1951	Now serving
	James H. Pipkin	Dec. 7, 1951	Now serving
GENERAL COUNSELS	Amos L. Beaty	Nov. 25, 1913	Mar. 23, 1920
	Edwin B. Parker	June 3, 1920	Mar. 27, 1923
	Charles B. Ames	Mar. 27, 1923	Dec. 28, 1925
	Harry T. Klein	Dec. 28, 1925	Apr. 25, 1944
	Oscar John Dorwin	Apr. 25, 1944	Now serving
SECRETARIES	Fred W. Freeman	May 20, 1902	June 13, 1905
	James L. Autry**	June 13, 1905	Nov. 25, 1913
	Clarence P. Dodge	Nov. 25, 1913	*Died Jan. 13, 1926*
	Edward M. Crone	Oct. 19, 1926	*Died June 20, 1938*
	Richard L. Saunders	June 24, 1938	Sept. 1, 1945
	Walter G. Elicker	Sept. 1, 1945	Now serving
TREASURERS	E. J. Marshall	May 20, 1902	Nov. 25, 1902
	Roderick Oliver	Nov. 25, 1902	Nov. 17, 1903
	Thomas J. Donoghue	Nov. 17, 1903	Nov. 29, 1907
	R. E. Brooks	Nov. 29, 1907	Jan. 1, 1913
	W. A. Green	Jan. 1, 1913	Nov. 14, 1916***
	W. W. Bruce	Apr. 1, 1920	Apr. 7, 1925
	C. E. Woodbridge	Apr. 7, 1925	June 30, 1939
	L. H. Lindeman	July 1, 1939	June 24, 1949
	Robert Fisher	June 24, 1949	Now serving
COMPTROLLERS	W. A. Green	Jan. 1, 1912	Jan. 1, 1913
	Ira McFarland	Jan. 1, 1913	Sept. 1, 1944
	Ernest C. Breeding	Sept. 1, 1944	Now serving

Elected Executive Vice President Jan. 26, 1951.
**Also served as General Attorney.*
***From Nov. 14, 1916, to Apr. 1, 1920, there was no elected Treasurer.*

CREDITS

Photographic illustrations in this book were selected from the archives of The Texas Company, with the following exceptions:

Page 14, A. Devaney, Inc. *(lower right)*; Page 69, Arabian American Oil Company *(top)*; Page 72, American Petroleum Institute *(center)*; Page 88, California Texas Oil Company, Limited *(top)*, Arabian American Oil Company *(bottom)*; Page 91, Arabian American Oil Company.

DESIGN:
Tobias Moss and
Ariosto Nardozzi

PHOTOENGRAVINGS:
Sterling Engraving Company

PRINTING:
The Condé Nast Press

BINDING:
J. F. Tapley Company

Faithfully Yours

1902 TEXACO 1952

for Fifty Years